Master English Grammar in 24 Hours

Michael J. Princeton
Susan D. Armstrong

Contents

Introduction

Why should I study grammar?   For one thing, doing so will enhance your ability to communicate. Logical, orderly expressions are, after all, easier to understand than illogical, disorderly ones. In addition, writing grammatically will encourage you to organize your thoughts and carefully consider what you're actually trying to say. That is, understanding grammar improves not only your expressions but also the thinking that underlies them.

Another reason: few people will take you or your writing seriously if you make obvious usage mistakes. Poor expression suggests ignorance, carelessness, and shoddy thinking in the same way that rigorous expression suggests knowledgeability, attentiveness, and intelligence.

Finally, people assume that sloppy writers will produce substandard work in general. Consider the following:

- CareerBuilder, which operates the largest employment website in the United States, conducted a nationwide survey of more than 2000 hiring managers. The survey indicates that 61% of employers would "automatically dismiss a candidate from consideration" because of typos on a résumé.
- In a Harvard Business Review article, CEO Kyle Wiens bluntly explained his willingness to reject qualified job applicants on the basis of grammatical errors, claiming (1) that people who don't care about writing tend to be flippant about other important things and (2) that "people who make fewer mistakes on a grammar test also make fewer mistakes when they are doing something completely unrelated to writing."

Who can use this book?   Any proficient English user who knows little about grammar. Being familiar with basic grammatical terminology helps, but it isn't crucial. We tried to achieve accessibility and compactness without resorting to oversimplification, so that even beginners could easily, quickly, and thoroughly understand even difficult concepts. To help particularly young readers, we included a very brief dictionary (starting on page 143). We hope it will make looking up unfamiliar terms more convenient for them.

Mastery in 24 hours? Really?   Yes, really. Even students new to the subject should achieve a thorough understanding of English grammar after 24 hours of study. Those already familiar with the main terms and concepts will take considerably less time.

Notice that "24 hours" refers to how much time you spend studying this book, not to how much time passes after you purchase it. The time you spend eating, sleeping, commuting, playing video games, etc. doesn't count toward the 24 hours.

Most students should easily be able to finish studying the book in a week or two. Completion in a few days is possible for the highly motivated (i.e. people cramming for standardized tests).

What does this book cover?   We addressed everything we thought a typical English user might need to know to construct logical, orderly expressions. A lot of the material, unfortunately, is simply not taught in schools or adequately addressed by books students normally use.

What does this book *not* cover?

- Since we're assuming the reader is a proficient speaker, the book doesn't specifically address idioms.
- This book isn't a style manual. It doesn't go into excruciating detail about when numbers should be expressed with words instead of digits, whether *the* should be considered part of a title, why some people write *A.M.* (but not *A.D.*) in small capitals, or whether a term should be hyphenated.
- We left out material we think has no practical value, even if other grammar books usually address it.

Can I use this book to prepare for the SAT or ACT?   Absolutely. Both have grammar portions. If you're short on time, we recommend skipping the following:

- proper use of ellipses (2.12)
- combining punctuation (2.14)
- spelling (A.1)

Neither test will ask you about usage theory or grammatical jargon. Almost every question focuses on your ability to spot serious errors or identify the best version of a phrase, sentence, or paragraph.

If you understand everything in this book, the grammar questions on the SAT or ACT will probably seem very easy to you.

What should I expect as I read this book?

- We tried to use tables and lists as much as we could in presenting material, because we thought doing so would make finding and reviewing information easier. With this format, students can more easily mark off things they already understand or highlight parts they wish to come back to.
- Some of our examples were built to illustrate how a grammatical rule would apply to an unusual situation. Contrived or noticeably awkward examples are not guides for how expressions should be constructed. Generally, we point out when rephrasing is a good idea.
- The most difficult concepts appear in section 1.1, so don't be discouraged if you have some trouble at first. The material gets a lot easier.
- We included a lot of grammatical terminology, but most of it is present so that people can look things up. Our advice is to focus on the concepts and not worry about the vocabulary. Understanding the ideas is far more important than memorizing the definitions.

I found a mistake, think something is unclear, or have some other suggestion for improving this book.
We would love to hear from you. You can reach us with the e-mail address in the appendix.

Chapter 1

Grammar

1.1 Verbs

Verbs express actions (e.g. *I run, I conclude, I think, I admire, I fear, I hope, I listen*) or states of being (e.g. *it is tall, they seem friendly, you feel sick*). A verb may consist of several words.

Example 1. Multi-word verbs

1. I **should have studied** more.
2. **Did** you **buy** anything?
3. I **may be going.**
4. I **have** not yet **finished.**

In example 1, *should, have, did, may,* and *be* are **auxiliaries** (also known as **helping verbs**). *Studied, buy, going,* and *finished* are **main verbs**.

Example 2. Auxiliaries you should be familiar with

1. is	7. being	13. does	19. may
2. am	8. been	14. did	20. might
3. are	9. has	15. shall	21. must
4. was	10. have	16. will	
5. were	11. had	17. should	22. can
6. be	12. do	18. would	23. could

Notice that in sentence 4 of example 1, *not* and *yet* are not part of the verb. They are actually **modifiers**. See section 1.2 for more information about modifiers.

Some auxiliaries can function as main verbs.

Example 3. Some auxiliaries that can function as main verbs

1. They are undefeated.
   Remark. Are is a main verb.

2. They are reading books.
   Remark. Are is an auxiliary in the verb *are reading*.

3. I have a sailboat.
   Remark. Have is a main verb.

4. I have finished my work.
   Remark. Have is an auxiliary in the verb *have finished*.

The **subjects** that correspond to a verb are the expressions that identify who or what is performing the action or state the verb describes. In example 3, *they* and *I* are subjects. See 1.11.1 for help with identifying subjects.

Subjects can contain all sorts of descriptive words, as example 4 shows.

Example 4.

Spending time with family is important.

Spending time with family is the **complete subject** of *is*. The complete subject includes a keyword called the **simple subject** (e.g. *spending* in example 4), as well as any expressions that modify or complement part of the complete subject (e.g. *time* and *with family* help specify what sort of spending is important). In discussions of grammar, the term *subject* usually refers to the simple subject.

There are six properties of verbs you should be familiar with.

1. Transitivity
2. Voice
3. Number
4. Person
5. Time
6. Mood

Below, we further discuss the six properties.

1.1.1 Transitivity

Transitive verbs direct actions at things (sometimes called **objects**); **intransitive** verbs do not. Some verbs can be used transitively or intransitively.

1. Transitive
   (a) I **smelled** the <u>food</u>.
   (b) I **tasted** the <u>water</u>.
   (c) **Sound** the <u>alarm</u>.

2. Intransitive
   (a) The food **smells** great.
   (b) The water **tasted** strange.
   (c) That **sounds** promising.

Other verbs that can be used transitively or intransitively include *feel, grow,* and *look.* Transitivity does not depend on whether an object is stated (e.g. *eaten* is a transitive verb in the sentence "I have not eaten for three hours").

Objects may be direct or indirect. A **direct object** is something the verb acts on. An **indirect object** is an entity the action is done for or done to. Objects are a kind of **complement**, something that completes the meaning of another expression. Recognizing complements is more important than distinguishing between different kinds.

Example 5. Complements

1. We sent them the new schedule.

   Remark. Them and *schedule* complement *sent.*

2. We held a meeting.

   Remark. Meeting complements *held.*

3. We named our cat Orion.

   Remark. Cat and *Orion* complement *named.*

4. It made them rich.

   Remark. Them and *rich* complement *made.*

Linking verbs are a kind of intransitive verb. *Appear, stay, remain,* and *seem,* as well as forms of *be* (*is, are, was, were,* etc.) are examples of linking verbs. *Smell, taste, sound, look,* and *feel,* which we mentioned earlier, are also linking verbs when used intransitively. A linking verb does not have objects; rather, it associates things (1) with descriptive words called **adjectives** or (2) with other things. The associated adjectives or things are the complements of the linking verb.

Example 6. Complements of linking verbs

1. You seem happy.

   Remark. Seem associates the noun *you* with the adjective *happy. Happy* complements the verb *seem.*

2. I am the supervisor.

   Remark. Am associates the noun *I* with the noun *supervisor. Supervisor* complements the verb *am.*

1.1.2 Voice

The subject of a verb in **active voice** acts upon something, whereas the subject of a verb in **passive voice** is being acted upon. Only transitive verbs have a passive form.

Example 7. Active and passive voice

1. The officer searched the entire area.

   Remark. Searched is an active verb.

2. The entire area has been searched.

   Remark. Has been searched is a passive verb.

Notice that *area*, the object in the active sentence, becomes the subject of the passive sentence. The one originally performing the action (i.e. the officer) is missing in the passive construction. To include the performer, use a **prepositional phrase** (e.g. *the entire area has been searched **by the officer***).

If an active statement involving multiple complements is converted to a passive statement, it may have something called a **retained object**.

Example 8. Retained objects

Remark. Sentences 2 and 3 are passive versions of 1.

1. They gave me an opportunity.

   Remark. *Me* and *opportunity* complement *gave*.

2. I was given an opportunity by them.

   Remark. *Opportunity* becomes a retained object while *me* becomes the subject.

3. An opportunity was given me by them.

   Remark. *Opportunity* becomes the subject while *me* becomes a retained object. "An opportunity was given to me by them" is less awkward.

Because direct, concise expressions are preferable to complicated, wordy ones, active constructions are generally preferable to passive ones. Don't use passive voice carelessly, but don't be afraid to use it if there's a good reason for it. Passive voice may be more appropriate in the following cases:

1. You wish to emphasize an action rather than its performer.
2. The identity of the performer is unknown, unimportant, or obvious.

1.1.3   Number and person

The **number** of a verb describes whether it expresses the action or state of one (a singular verb) or many (a plural verb). **Person** describes whether a verb corresponds to the writer (i.e. is first person), the one being addressed (i.e. is second person), or a third party (i.e. is third person).

Table 1.1.1 shows how various verbs change depending on number and person.

Table 1.1.1: Forms of *be*, *have*, and *do*

	Singular	Plural
First person	(I) was/am | have | do	(we) were/are | have | do
Second person	(you) were/are | have | do	(you) were/are | have | do
Third person	(he, she, it) was/is | has | does	(they) were/are | have | do

Had and *did* do not change form based on person or number.

Most of the time, person affects the form of a verb only when it is singular and in present time. Generally, you must add *–s* to the base form of a verb to create the third person, singular, present form.

Table 1.1.2: Forms of *work*

	Singular	Plural
First person	(I) work	(we) work
Second person	(you) work	(you) work
Third person	(he, she, it) **works**	(they) work

If you are referring to present time with *do*, then it changes instead of the main verb.

Table 1.1.3: Forms of *do work*

	Singular	Plural
First person	(I) do work	(we) do work
Second person	(you) do work	(you) do work
Third person	(he, she, it) **does work**	(they) do work

1.1.4 Time

1.1.4.1 Time period descriptions

English verbs refer to different periods of time through a combination of auxiliaries and changes in form. There are three main time periods: past, present, and future.

For each main time period, there is a **perfect time period**. Thus, there are six periods you should be familiar with:

1. Past perfect: actions or states that occur before other past actions or states
2. Past: completed actions or states
3. Present perfect: actions or states that began in the past and continue into the present
4. Present: actions or states occurring now
5. Future perfect: future actions or states that occur before other future actions or states
6. Future: actions or states that will occur later

For each time period you refer to, you can use a **progressive form** to emphasize continuing action. A progressive form makes use of the present participle of a verb (the form that ends in *-ing*) and a form of the verb *be*.

Table 1.1.4 demonstrates forms of the 12 temporal configurations (six time periods, both progressive and non-progressive). The bold temporal forms have the same structure regardless of person or number — that is, the form of the verb is always the same.

Table 1.1.4: Temporal forms

Time	Form(s)	Examples
past perfect	**[had] + past participle**	had written | had walked
past perfect progressive	**[had been] + present participle**	had been writing | had been walking
past	**past form**	wrote | walked
	[did] + base form	did write | did walk
	present perfect forms	I have written. | It has walked.

past progressive	[was/were] + present participle	I was writing.	They were walking.
present perfect	[has/have] + past participle	I have written.	It has walked.
present perfect progressive	[has/have] + [been] + present participle	I have been writing.	It has been walking.
present	base form (add -s for third person singular)	I write.	It walks.
	[do/does] + base form	I do write.	It does walk.
present progressive	[is/am/are] + present participle	I am writing.	They are walking.
future perfect	**[will have] + past participle**	will have written	will have walked
future perfect progressive	**[will have been] + present participle**	will have been writing	will have been walking
future	**[will] + base form**	will write	will walk
	present forms	I leave tomorrow.
future progressive	**[will be] + present participle**	will be writing	will be walking
	present progressive forms	They are competing next week.

If several auxiliaries are available to construct a particular form (e.g. present progressive), choose the auxiliary that properly expresses the intended person and number (see table 1.1.1).

Notice that you can refer to future time in more than one way (e.g. using the base form of a verb or using the auxiliary *will*). Also note that *will* does not always indicate future time.

Example 9.

Walk this way, if you will.

Remark. Will expresses willingness in this example.

Could, might, should, and *would* can function as the past forms of *can, may, shall,* and *will,* respectively. For guidelines about using particular auxiliaries, see 3.5.9.

If a verb is passive, refer to a time by using what would ordinarily be the progressive form, but use a past participle (i.e. the form that usually ends in *–ed*) instead of a present participle (i.e. the *–ing* form). For example, *had been repaired* would be the passive past perfect form of *repair*. Add *being* to make a passive verb progressive (e.g. *is being repaired, was being repaired*).

1.1.4.2   Principal parts

In order to construct all the forms in table 1.1.4, you must know the principal parts of a verb: the **base form**, the **present participle**, the **past form**, and the **past participle**.

1. To form the present participle of a verb, add *-ing* to the end of the base form.
2. Generally, construct the past form and the past participle by adding *-ed* to the end of the base form.

(Note: the appendix has guidelines for spelling participles.)

Table 1.1.5 shows the principal parts of some ordinary verbs.

Table 1.1.5: Principal parts of some ordinary verbs

Base form	Present participle	Past form	Past participle
dive	diving	dived	dived
drag	dragging	dragged	dragged
dream	dreaming	dreamed	dreamed
drug	drugging	drugged	drugged

Many verbs, unlike those in table 1.1.5, have irregular past forms or irregular past participles. Table 1.1.6 shows some common irregular verbs. A more comprehensive table appears in the appendix.

Table 1.1.6: Common irregular verbs

Base form	Past form	Past participle
be	was/were	been
bet	bet	bet
bring	brought (not *brang*)	brought (not *brung*)
cling	clung	clung
drink	drank	drunk
hang (capital punishment)	hanged	hanged
hang	hung	hung
lay	laid	laid
lead	led	led
lie	lay	lain
sink	sank	sunk
swim	swam	swum
write	wrote	written
get	got	got, gotten
shrink	shrank	shrunk

1.1.4.3 Guidelines for placing verbs in the proper time

1. Select a point in time to serve as your reference, then describe each action or state in a temporal form that accurately depicts when it happens relative to your reference point.

Example 10. Each sentence below changes meaning depending on which verbs are chosen from its bracketed groups.

1. My friend [saw | sees | will see] the same landmarks that I [saw | see | will see].
2. They [explained | are explaining | will explain] the construction that [took | is taking | will take] place.
3. Your friends [said | say | will say] that they [worried | worry | will worry] about you.
4. Several weeks ago, they predicted that they [would | will] win the game.

Example 11 demonstrates the meanings achieved by combining verbs of various times.

Example 11.

1. My friend saw the same landmarks that I had seen.

   Remark. We saw the same landmarks in the past; I saw them before my friend did.

2. My friend saw the same landmarks that I saw.

   Remark. We saw the same landmarks in the past. We might have seen them at the same time, but the order is unspecified.

3. My friend saw the same landmarks that I see.

   Remark. I am currently looking at the same landmarks that my friend already saw.

4. My friend saw the same landmarks that I will see.

   Remark. My friend has already seen the landmarks, but I have not. I will see them later.

5. My friend will see the same landmarks that I saw.

   Remark. I have already seen the landmarks, and my friend will see them later.

6. My friend will see the same landmarks that I see.

   Remark. My friend will see the landmarks in the future. I am either looking at the landmarks now, or I will also see them in the future. Who sees the landmarks first is unspecified.

7. My friend will see the same landmarks that I will see.

   Remark. We both unambiguously see the landmarks in the future. Who sees them first is unspecified.

8. My friend will see the same landmarks that I will have seen.

   Remark. We both see the landmarks in the future, and I see them before my friend does.

9. Several weeks ago, they predicted that they will win the game.

   Remark. From the perspective of the writer, the prediction has already occurred, but the game has not.

10. Several weeks ago, they predicted that they would win the game.

    Remark. Probably, the game is already over from the writer's perspective. However, because *would* doesn't necessarily refer to the past, the sentence could also describe a game that has not yet occurred.

You can describe past events or fictional events in present time to create the sense that they are happening now.

Example 12. Writing fiction in the present

Fear, that relentless pursuer, hinders Dantes's efforts. He listens for any sound that might be audible, and every time that he rises to the top of the water, he scans the horizon and strives to peer through the darkness. He imagines that every wave behind him is a pursuing boat, and he redoubles his efforts, rapidly increasing his distance from the prison but exhausting his strength. He swims on still, and already the terrible dungeon has disappeared in the darkness. He can not see it, but he feels its presence. An hour passes, during which Dantes, excited by the feeling of freedom, continues to struggle through the waves.

Maintain the same reference point throughout your writing unless you have a good reason to change. In the next example, everything was originally in past time. We've changed some words (the bold ones) so that there is an unnecessary shift to present time.

Example 13. Unnecessary changes in time

They all made a rush at Alice the moment she **appears**; but she **runs** off as fast as she **can** and soon found herself safe in a dense forest.

After beginning with the perspective that the events are finished, there is no reason to suddenly write in present time and then return to writing in past time.

Sometimes, a change in temporal perspective is reasonable. Consider example 14.

Example 14. Too many past perfect verbs

My friends told me that they **had** missed their second flight because the plane they **had** first boarded **had** been delayed. They **had** at first been concerned, but a representative of the airline **had** assured them that he **had** been trying to find another way for them to get to their destination. After a few moments, he **had** told them that he **had** successfully found them an alternative. Soon after, they **had** retrieved their belongings and **had** successfully departed.

The past verb *told* causes many of the subsequent verb forms to be perfect. In a situation like this, changing perspective makes the writing much smoother. In example 15, we will shift perspective by saying *they were at first concerned* instead of *they had at first been concerned*. The subsequent verbs can then be in past time.

Example 15. A helpful change in temporal perspective

My friends told me that they had missed their second flight because the plane they had first boarded had been delayed. They **were** at first concerned, but a representative of the airline **assured** them that he **had been trying** to find another way for them to get to their destination. After a few moments, he **told** them that he **had** successfully **found** them an alternative. Soon after, they **retrieved** their belongings and successfully **departed**.

Notice that after we shift to ordinary past time, we are once again able to use past perfect forms to distinguish the order of past events.

If you're going to shift perspective, do so early on. Also try not to change perspective in the middle of a sentence.

2. Make the order of events clear whenever doing so is required logically or is important to the meaning of your statement.

- Use past perfect time solely to clarify the order of multiple past events, and use future perfect time solely to clarify the order of multiple future events. **Specifying order is the only purpose for which past perfect or future perfect time should be used**.

- When using past perfect to order multiple past events, describe in past perfect time all but the most recent past occurrence, which should be described in ordinary past time.

- When using future perfect to order multiple future occurrences, use the future perfect form to describe all but the latest occurrence (i.e. the one that occurs furthest in the future), which should be described in future time.

Example 16.

1. The others finally arrived, but we left and were asked to start without them.

   Remark. Everything happened in the past; the order is not specified.

2. The others finally arrived, but we had left and had been asked to start without them.

   Remark. Their arrival occurred after all the other past events. The order of the two past perfect actions is unspecified.

3. We will prepare the food, and they will put up the decorations.

   Remark. Two events occur in the future, without any order being specified.

4. Before you arrive tomorrow, we will have prepared the food, and they will have put up the decorations.

   Remark. Your arrival occurs in the future, after two other future events. The order of the two future perfect actions is unspecified.

5. I reviewed the report you had written.

   Remark. Logically, the writing of the report must occur before the reviewing of the report, so the past perfect form *had written* is correct.

6. The discovery caused a wave of public excitement I had never seen.

   Remark. Logically, never seeing such a wave of public excitement must have occurred before seeing such a wave of public excitement. Therefore, the past perfect form *had seen* is appropriate.

7. Before the sun rises again, it will have set.

   Remark. The sun must set before it can rise again, so the future perfect form *will have set* must be used.

8. I had stretched and had exercised.

   Remark. The order of past events is not being specified, so usage of the past perfect is unnecessary. "I stretched and exercised" is better.

9. We will discuss the report you will write.

   Remark. The order of events is important but unspecified. The sentence should be rewritten so that the reader understands when *write* occurs relative to *discuss* (e.g. *we will discuss the report you will have written*).

- Modifiers can order events as well. Modifiers must be used if you wish to specify the order of events that are already described in past perfect or future perfect time.

Example 17. Using modifiers to clarify the order of perfect verbs

1. I **had changed** majors three times **after** I **had** twice **transferred** schools, but I finally graduated.
2. By the time you arrive, we **will have prepared** the food, just **before** they **will have finished** decorating.

- Even if modifiers already make the order of events clear, use perfect forms that are consistent with the meaning of your statement as long as doing so is not awkward.

Example 18. Using perfect forms and modifiers together

1. Before we constructed the prototype, we had carefully considered its design.
2. I departed shortly after you had arrived.
3. Before you arrive, I will have departed.

- Perfect forms, however, are not required to specify order. Don't bother using a perfect form if doing so is awkward and if the order of events is already clear.

Example 19.

1. After I had had some time to think, I answered the question.
   Remark. awkward use of the past perfect

2. After I had some time to think, I answered the question.
   Remark. Using the ordinary past sounds better. *After* makes the order of events clear.

3. I will review the report that you will have written.
   Remark. awkward use of the future perfect

4. I will review the report that you write.
   Remark. Using ordinary future sounds better. Obviously, the reviewing must occur after the writing.

3. Use the present perfect form to describe actions or states that began in the past and continue in the present. The present perfect form can also describe completed actions or states, just as the past form can. When using a present perfect form, ensure that the reader can determine whether you are describing a completed action or a continuing one.

Example 20. Present perfect verbs

1. I **have been preparing** since yesterday.
   Remark. a past action that continues to the present

2. I **have lived** here for over 50 years.
   Remark. a past action that continues to the present

3. I **have eaten** breakfast already.
   Remark. a completed past action

4. The school **has worked** to change this policy.
   Remark. The sentence is unclear. The reader cannot be sure whether the school continues to work in the present or whether the work was finished a long time ago. "The school worked to change this policy" and "the school has been working to change this policy" are clearer.

4. Use a present form unless there is an obvious reason to use another one.

Example 21. Using present forms

1. One **is** greater than zero.
   Remark. an eternal truth

2. I **am** tired every morning.
   Remark. a regular occurrence

3. I often **become** nervous before going on stage.
   Remark. a tendency

1.1.5   Mood

Verbs take on one of three moods — indicative, imperative, and subjunctive.

1. **Indicative** mood is used unless there is a reason to use one of the other two moods. All the verbs in the previous sentence (and in this one) are indicative.

2. **Imperative** verbs express requests or commands.

Example 22. Imperative verbs

1. **Be** careful.
2. **Prepare** yourself.
3. **Pay** attention.
4. **Do** not **eat** that.

5. **Do** not **be** ridiculous.
6. **Let** us begin.
7. Nobody **move**!
8. Somebody please **help**.

- The subject of an imperative verb is the one being addressed and is often unstated. The subject, if unstated, is known as **you understood**.
- A verb's imperative form is the same as its base form.
- Construct negative commands by using the auxiliary *do* and the modifier *not*.

3. **Subjunctive** verbs express states or actions the writer understands to be **unreal** or **contrary to fact**, such as those generally found in wishes, demands, suggestions, and hypothetical statements.

Example 23. Subjunctive verbs

1. The teacher suggested that the student **prepare** for the examination.
   Remark. The sentence implies that the student is not preparing.

2. The teacher suggested that the student **be** prepared for the examination.

3. The students demanded that they **be evaluated** fairly.
   Remark. The sentence implies that the students are not evaluated fairly.

Notice how the subjunctive verbs associated with *student* differ from indicative ones. In the indicative mood, you would say *the student prepares, the student is prepared,* and *they are evaluated fairly* — not *the student prepare, the student be prepared,* or *they be evaluated fairly.*

1.1.5.1 How to use the subjunctive

1. Use the indicative past perfect form (i.e. *had* + past participle) to express past time in the subjunctive mood.
2. Use the base form or the indicative past form to express non-past time in the subjunctive mood.
3. Don't use *was* as a subjunctive form of *be.* Use *were* instead.

Example 24.

1. The drought finally ended, but I wish it **had ended** sooner.
   Remark. The drought is already over, but the speaker thinks it was too long.

2. I wish the sun **were shining**.
   Remark. There is currently no sunlight, and the speaker wants there to be some right now.

3. I wish I **could get** more work done.
   Remark. The speaker is currently incapable of getting more work done.

4. I wish they **would give** me an answer.
   Remark. They are not ever going to provide an answer.

5. They wish they **knew** more about computers.
   Remark. They currently don't know anything about computers.

6. They wish they **had studied** more in school.
   Remark. They are finished with school. While they were there, they studied very little.

---

4. Subjunctive base forms (such as those in demands or suggestions) can refer to any time period.

Example 25. Subjunctive forms with demands or suggestions

1. I ask that they **be** released now.
2. I ask that they **be** released tomorrow.
3. I had asked that they **be** released before today.
4. I will ask that they **be** released.

Remark. In these example sentences, *be* is the proper subjunctive form regardless of what time it refers to.

---

5. When expressing the consequences of subjunctive conditionals, keep in mind the following guidelines:

   (a) Use *would* for non-past consequences.
   (b) Use *would have* for past consequences.

Example 26. Consequences of subjunctive conditionals

1. If I **drove**, we **would get** home safely. If he **drove**, we **would be** in danger.
   Remark. non-past subjunctive conditionals followed by non-past subjunctive consequences

2. If I **were driving**, we **would get** home safely. If he **were driving**, we **would be** in danger.
   Remark. non-past subjunctive conditionals followed by non-past subjunctive consequences

3. If I **had driven**, we **would have gotten** home safely. If he **had driven**, we **would have been** in danger.
   Remark. past subjunctive conditionals followed by past subjunctive consequences

4. If I **had been incinerated** by a bolt of lightning yesterday, I **would** not **be talking** to you now.
   Remark. a past subjunctive conditional followed by a non-past subjunctive consequence

5. If I **had** more time, I **would go** swimming.
   Remark. Here, *had* is a non-past subjunctive verb meaning *possessed*. It is not an auxiliary.

Usually, the time sequences you will see are as follows:

1. Subjunctive verbs that look like the indicative past, followed by *would* (e.g. *If X were, then Y would.*)
2. Subjunctive verbs that look like the indicative past perfect, followed by *would have* (e.g. *If X had, then Y would have.*)

Remember that logic determines correct use; a sequence does not have to conform to one of the two we just described (e.g. sentence 4 of example 26 does not follow either). To sequence subjunctive verbs properly, determine what time periods the condition and consequence should logically refer to, then use the appropriate temporal forms.

People normally express a condition and its consequence in different forms, as in "if I exercise more, then I will be healthier." You probably wouldn't say "if I will exercise more, then I will be healthier," so don't say "if they would have exercised more, then they would have been healthier." Generally, *would* should not be used in the condition but can be used in the consequence.

Example 27.

1. If the drought were over, I would drink some water.
2. If I had stared at the sun, I would have gone blind.
3. If I had stared at the sun, I would be blind.

However, if *would* expresses something in present time (e.g. willingness), the word can be used in the conditional part of the statement.

Example 28.

If you would just listen to me, all your questions would be answered.

1.1.5.2 When to use the subjunctive

Not all statements involving *if* require the subjunctive mood. Do not use subjunctive mood when using *if* to express undetermined possibilities.

Example 29.

1. If the drought ends, I will drink some water.
   Remark. No one knows whether the drought will end.

2. If I drive, we will get home safely. If he drives, we will be in danger.
   Remark. Who will drive has not yet been determined.

3. If the team was unprepared, no one noticed.
   Remark. The speaker does not know whether the team was prepared.

The subjunctive is almost never required in future conditionals. They cannot logically be contrary to fact unless you are certain of what the future holds. Besides, why bother with the subjunctive unless you absolutely have to? Change the form of a verb only with good reason.

Example 30. Using indicative mood instead of subjunctive mood

1. If something unusual were to happen tomorrow...
   Remark. The subjunctive is unnecessary.

2. If something unusual should happen tomorrow...
   Remark. The subjunctive is unnecessary.

3. If something unusual happens tomorrow...
   Remark. The verb is indicative. Here, an indicative verb more simply expresses the intended meaning, even if the subjunctive is justifiable.

Subjunctive forms can play an important role in clarifying whether the author is writing about possibility or unreality.

Example 31.

1. Indicative: The animal behaves as if it is frightened.
   Remark. The animal is possibly frightened, but the writer doesn't know.

2. Subjunctive: The animal behaves as if it were frightened.
   Remark. The animal is not actually frightened.

3. Indicative: They act as if their crimes will be excused.
   Remark. There is a chance they will be excused.

4. Subjunctive: They act as if their crimes would be excused.
   Remark. They will be punished for their crimes.

Since the mood of a verb can change the meaning of a sentence, be sure to use the subjunctive if and only if a situation actually calls for it.

Example 32.   Assume that *thought* is subjunctive. Which verb in brackets should follow it?

If they thought our planet [is | were | was] flat, they would act differently.

In example 32, the thinking — not the description of the thought — is contrary to fact. Yes, our planet isn't flat, but we're not speaking as though it were. *Our planet is flat* correctly describes the thought they don't think. The unreal condition in our sentence isn't *if our planet were flat*. The unreal condition is *if they thought*.

Therefore, *thought* being subjunctive makes sense, but there's no reason to make the verb in *our planet is flat* subjunctive. The sentence should be *if they thought our planet is flat, they would act differently*.

If they thought our planet was flat is acceptable as well, but it seems to mean *if they thought our planet used to be flat and no longer is*.

Logically combining subjunctive and indicative verbs can sound strange, and often, wordings that sound good are hard to justify. Consider rewriting if you find yourself choosing between sounding right and being logical. Example 33 demonstrates one way of rewording *if they thought our planet is flat, they would act differently*.

Example 33.   Rewriting an awkward subjunctive

They would act differently if they didn't know that our planet is round.

Remark.   Separating the subjunctive *would act* from the indicative *is* keeps the sentence from sounding awkward. Also, because *know* looks like a present indicative, it doesn't sound strange next to *is*.

Remember that what is "not real" is determined by what the writer assumes to be false — not necessarily what is actually false.

Example 34.

Person A: I'm trying to help you.

Person B: If that were true, you would stop talking and start digging.

Remark.   Even if person A really is trying to help, the second sentence uses the subjunctive because person B is speaking with the assumption that person A is not trying to help.

The following three-step process can help you use mood and time properly:

1. Determine what mood the verb should be. Consult the guidelines from 1.1.5.2 for help on whether a verb should be subjunctive.

2. Decide what time the verb should refer to so that it correctly conveys your intended meaning. The time period descriptions in 1.1.4.1 will help you.

3. Determine what form correctly expresses the mood and time you chose. Tables 1.1.4 (page 11) and 1.1.1 (page 10), as well as guidelines from 1.1.5.1 and 1.1.4.3, should help.

Example 35. Choosing mood and time

I wished this machine worked as I had intended.

Remark. *Wished* is past indicative. You could also say *wish* or *will wish* depending on what time period the wishing occurs in.

Remark. *Worked* is present subjunctive. You could also say *had worked* or *would work* depending on what time period you want the working to occur in.

Remark. *Had intended,* a past perfect indicative verb, indicates intentions that existed before the wishing occurred. You could say *intended* to indicate that your intending coincides in the past with your wishing, and you could also say *intend* to indicate that your intention exists in the present.

1.2 Modifiers

1.2.1 Adjectives

Adjectives, which modify nouns, answer questions such as:

- Which?
- What kind?
- How many?

Example 36. Adjectives

1. Which?
   - (a) **those** hats
   - (b) **their** hats
   - (c) **every** hat

2. What kind?
   - (a) a **blue** hat
   - (b) an **old** hat
   - (c) a **unique** hat

3. How many?
   - (a) **several** hats
   - (b) **three** hats
   - (c) **many** hats

1. *Which* and *what* are themselves modifiers.
2. *A, an,* and *the* are special modifiers called **articles**. *The,* called the **definite article**, describes a particular thing. *A* and *an,* called **indefinite articles**, describe an unspecified member of some category.
3. Which indefinite article you use depends on the beginning sound of the immediately following word. Use *a* if the immediately following word starts with a consonant sound; use *an* if the immediately following word starts with a vowel sound. Note that what matters is the sound — not the letter — the word starts with. Choosing between *a* and *an* in a particular situation is really a matter of selecting which one sounds better .

Example 37. Choosing between *a* and *an*

1. an honorable person
2. a hungry animal
3. a historic moment
4. a universal symbol
5. an unethical person
6. a limited liability company
7. an LLC

   Remark. *LLC* begins with an *e* sound.

4. Sometimes, you will see adjectives that describe the subject of a sentence follow a linking verb such as *is*, *feel*, or *seem*.

Example 38.

   1. I <u>feel</u> **bad**.   2. It <u>is</u> **amazing**.   3. **They** <u>seem</u> **friendly**.

5. Present participles and past participles can function as adjectives.

Example 39.

   1. Students face **increasing** costs.   2. **Increased** costs are a problem for students.
     Remark. Increasing modifies *costs*.   *Remark. Increased* modifies *costs*.

6. A **participle phrase** includes a participle and can include any related complements, conjunctions, and modifiers.

Example 40. A participle phrase

Cheerfully giving our good friends expensive gifts, we smiled.

In example 40:

- *Our* and *good* modify *friends*.

- *Expensive* modifies *gifts*.

- *Giving* is a present participle that modifies *we*.

- *Cheerfully* is an adverb that modifies *giving*.

- *Friends* complements *giving*. (It's an **indirect object**.)

- *Gifts* complements *giving*. (It's a **direct object**.)

- *Cheerfully giving our good friends expensive gifts* is a **participle phrase**.

1.2.2 Adverbs

Adverbs, which modify modifiers and verb forms, answer questions such as:

- How?
- When?
- Where?
- Why?
- To what extent?

Example 41. Adverbs

1. How?

    (a) We walked **quickly**.
    (b) We **often** go on vacation.

2. When?

    (a) The weather is **always** pleasant.
    (b) I will retire **soon**.
    (c) We start **tomorrow**.

3. Where?

    (a) We searched **everywhere**.
    (b) We flew **over the Pacific**.

4. Why?

    (a) I work **to help others**.
    (b) I fight **for justice**.

5. To what extent?

    (a) The water is **too** hot.
    (b) The situation is **quite** complicated.
    (c) The process is **almost** finished.

1. *How, when, where,* and *why* can themselves be adverbs. They often appear in questions.

2. Adverbs commonly end in *–ly*, but there are many words that end in *–ly* that are not adverbs (e.g. *lively, friendly, silly, lovely*). There are also many adverbs that do not end in *-ly.*

3. Some words (e.g. *fast*) can function as adjectives or adverbs.

4. Remember that linking verbs can associate nouns with adjectives but not with adverbs.

Example 42.

1. The **water** looks **calm**.

    Remark. Calm describes *water*, not *look. Look* is a linking verb that associates *water* with *calm*. Water does not "look calmly."

2. **They** feel **bad** about what happened.

    Remark. Bad describes an emotional state, not how the emotion is experienced. The adjective *bad* is appropriate because it ultimately associates with *they* rather than with *feel. Feel* is the linking verb that connects *bad* to *they*. Try replacing *bad* with *guilty* if you have trouble understanding this example.

    Because *feel* can also be a transitive verb, you can also say *they feel badly*. However, *they feel badly* means they are unskilled at using their sense of touch. "They feel badly about what happened" is wrong.

3. They **feel strongly** about this matter.

    Remark. To say "they feel strong about this matter" is incorrect. The people are not themselves strong. Rather, they experience an emotion in a strong manner. Therefore, the adverb *strongly* is the proper form.

4. **I** feel **strong** after resting.

    Remark. What is strong? It is the person, not the way "feel" is performed. Therefore, the adjective *strong* is the proper form. "I feel strongly after resting" is incorrect.

5. My arm **hurts badly**.

    Remark. Badly describes how the hurting occurs, not the arm itself. Therefore, the adverb *badly* is the correct form.

1.2.3 Comparison

Modifiers take different forms when you make comparisons.

Table 1.2.1: Modifiers in comparisons

Form	Situation	General structure
Comparative	comparing two things	[less/more] + modifier modifier + [-er]
Superlative	comparing more than two things	[least/most] + modifier modifier + [-est]

The ordinary form of a modifier (i.e. with no comparison) is called ***positive***.

To decide between *more* and *-er* or *most* and *-est*, select the version that sounds better. For example, use *sloppiest* instead of *most sloppy*, use *prettiest* instead of *most pretty*, and use *most admirable* instead of *admirablest*. Choosing what is less awkward usually boils down to using *-er* or *-est* with monosyllabic words and using *more* or *most* otherwise. Consult a dictionary if you are unsure about the comparative or superlative form of a modifier. The appendix has guidelines for spelling comparative and superlative forms.

Some modifiers have irregular comparative or irregular superlative forms. Table 1.2.2 presents some examples.

Table 1.2.2: Irregular comparative and superlative words

Positive	Comparative	Superlative
bad, badly, ill	worse	worst
far	farther/further	farthest/furthest
good, well	better	best
little (amount, not size)	less	least
many, much, some	more	most

Example 43.

1. Wrong: It is one of the **most well-established** theories in science.
2. Right: It is one of the **best-established** theories in science.

Some modifiers do not have comparative or superlative forms. Called **absolute modifiers**, they describe qualities for which there are no degrees (e.g. *essential, ultimate, categorical, unique, empty, superior, fatal, perfect, impossible, omnipotent*). *Almost as perfect, less essential,* and *more unique* are all illogical expressions.

- *Perfect* means *having no flaws*. Something cannot "have no flaws" to a greater degree than something else "has no flaws" — it either has flaws or it doesn't. However, something can be "closer to perfect" than something else.

- If an engine requires component A and component B to work, then both components are essential. One cannot be "less essential" than the other one — if either part breaks, the engine will not work. Something can be "less important" than something else, however.

- *Unique* means *one of a kind*. There are no degrees of being the only one. Something can be "rarer" or "more peculiar" than something else, but it can't be "more unique."

There are no degrees of an absolute quality, but something can approach an absolute quality to a greater or lesser degree.

Example 44. Absolute modifiers

1. Wrong: The first container is emptier than the second one.
2. Right: The first container is closer to empty than the second one.
3. Right: The first container is more nearly empty than the second one.

Remark. "The first container has less than the second one" is better.

1.2.4 Additional notes about modifiers

1. Use *farther* and *farthest* only when referring to physical distance (e.g. *I do not want to run any farther*). *Further* and *furthest* can refer to extent of any kind, including physical distance. (e.g. *I do not want to run any further*, *I do not want to discuss this any further*).
2. Use *many*, *few*, *fewer*, and *fewest* with things considered individually (e.g. dollars, buildings, pencils, molecules, people). Use *much*, *little*, *less*, and *least* with things thought of as a whole (e.g. money, time, water, air, optimism). This guideline is essentially about deciding which word sounds better. We recommend always following it in formal writing, though *less* is becoming acceptable in situations that traditionally call for *fewer* (e.g. *less people* can be used instead of *fewer people*).

Example 45. *Less* and *fewer*

1. Thousands of **students** apply each year, but **fewer** than 1% of them are admitted.
2. **Less** than 3% of the **water** has evaporated.

3. Do not use *less*, *least*, *more*, or *most* with a word that already expresses comparison (e.g. do not say *more faster*). Be aware that some words express comparison even though they do not end in *–er* or *–est*.

Example 46.

1. Wrong: Of those two choices, the second is more preferable.
2. Right: Of those two choices, the second is preferable.
3. Right: Of those three choices, the second is preferable to the first, and the third is even more preferable.
   Remark. Here, we can say *more preferable* because we are comparing how preferable two choices are to a third choice.

4. Negatives such as *not*, *never*, and *hardly* function as modifiers.
5. Capitalize modifiers that are based on proper nouns (e.g. **European** history, **Chinese** proverb, the **United States** government, **Caesar** salad).

6. Sometimes, you may see nouns function as modifiers (e.g. **science** *teacher*, **water** *treatment*, **sky** *blue*, **can** *opener*).

7. Sentence modifiers apply to the rest of their clause or sentence. If you use a sentence modifier, we recommend making it an adjective unless doing so is awkward.

Example 47. Sentence modifiers

1. **Naturally**, we won by a large margin.

   Remark. Naturally modifies *we won by a large margin*, not *won*. What would *naturally winning* even be?

2. The villains, **regrettably**, have completed their secret weapon.

   Remark. Regrettably does not modify *completed*. It modifies the rest of the clause and reflects the view of the speaker.

3. **First**, no one could have predicted it. **Second**, no one could have prepared for it.

4. They were, **amazingly**, prepared for the surprise examination.

   Remark. Notice that the meaning of the sentence changes if the commas are removed. *Amazingly* then modifies *prepared* instead of the rest of the sentence.

5. **The work having been completed**, we took a break.

6. **The work completed**, we took a break.

---

8. Modifiers do not always precede what they describe.

9. Be careful when placing modifiers, ensuring that they can modify only what you intend for them to. Otherwise, confusion or unintended meaning may result. See 3.1 for further discussion.

1.3   Prepositions

1. Prepositions express relationships.

Example 48. Common prepositions

1. about	7. around	13. between	19. into	25. past	31. with
2. above	8. at	14. despite	20. like	26. through	32. within
3. across	9. before	15. during	21. of	27. to	33. without
4. after	10. behind	16. for	22. on	28. toward	
5. against	11. below	17. from	23. on to	29. under	
6. among	12. besides	18. in	24. over	30. until	

---

2. A **prepositional phrase** includes a preposition and can include any related complements, conjunctions, and modifiers (e.g. *we slid **across the frozen lake***). Prepositional phrases generally function as modifiers.

3. Many prepositions are words that have other functions (e.g. *after* and *until* can function as conjunctions).

4. You can place prepositions wherever you want as long as your writing doesn't become awkward or unclear. Ignore the nonsensical claim that sentences shouldn't end with prepositions. Often, what seems to be

a preposition is actually an adverb (e.g. *we **wandered around**; we **put** some decorations **up***). Insisting that they can't come at the end of a sentence will sometimes lead you to write something ridiculous.

Example 49.

Awkward: We noticed the way around in which they walked.

Better: We noticed the way they walked around.

Awkward: It's something off without which you are better.

Better: It's something you're better off without.

1.4 Nouns

A noun names something.

Example 50. Nouns

1. Albert Einstein	8. entropy	15. family
2. Antarctica	9. hiking	16. team
3. audience	10. laser	17. president
4. chair	11. Mars	18. rock and roll
5. citizens	12. mathematics	19. *Romeo and Juliet*
6. criteria	13. Michelangelo	20. United States of America
7. data	14. multitude	21. wilderness

Notice from example 50 that:

1. A noun sometimes consists of more than one word.
2. Some nouns are capitalized. Called **proper nouns**, they are the titles of particular things or people. A noun that is not proper is **common**.

When dealing with proper nouns involving more than one word, capitalize the first word and the last word, as well as other "important" words. Prepositions, conjunctions, and articles are generally considered unimportant.

Example 51. Distinguishing between proper and common nouns

1. Common: doctor
2. Proper: Dr. Irving
3. Common: day
4. Proper: Sunday
5. Common: month
6. Proper: January

Example 52. Distinguishing between proper and common nouns

1. Common: That person is the president of the organization.
   Remark. The term *president* refers to a position in an organization.

2. Proper: Last week, President Washington made the announcement.
   Remark. President Washington is someone's title.

3. Proper: Soon, the President will give a speech.
   Remark. We are using *President* as someone's title.

4. Common: That is a principal's responsibility.
   Remark. We are not using *principal* as a title of a specific person.

5. Proper: The Principal visited us the other day.
   Remark. Principal is the title we are using to refer to a particular person.

6. Common: Our location is south of yours.
   Remark. South is just a direction, not a title.

7. Proper: We got to see the South Pole.
   Remark. South Pole is the title of a particular location.

There are four properties of nouns you should be familiar with.

1. Number   2. Case   3. Person   4. Gender

1.4.1   Number: singular or plural

Number describes whether a noun refers to one or many.

1. A singular noun names one thing. A plural noun names more than one thing.

2. A collective noun is singular even though it names something with many elements. For example, *family* is singular despite comprising several people, because it is considered a unit. Other collective nouns include *audience, crowd, team, group, fleet, committee, class, chorus, jury, orchestra, furniture*, and *herd*.

3. You can treat a collective noun as plural to refer to its elements. For example, you could write "the jury were in disagreement," though "the members of the jury were in disagreement" is preferable.

4. Study the spelling guidelines in the appendix if you are having trouble forming plurals.

5. There are many nouns that have irregular plurals or other unusual numerical properties. Table 1.4.1 contains some examples.

Table 1.4.1: Numerically unusual words

Singular	Plural
child	children
foot	feet
sheep	sheep

moose	moose
shrimp	shrimp
fish	fish
(no singular)	clothes
(no singular)	scissors
(no singular)	police
physics (field of study)	**(no plural)**
criterion	criteria
passer-by	passers-by
mother-in-law	mothers-in-law
get-together	get-togethers
good-for-nothing	good-for-nothings
mouse	mice
louse	lice
deer	deer
goose	geese
crisis	crises
curriculum	curricula
appendix	appendices
dust	**(no plural)**
honesty	**(no plural)**
oxygen	**(no plural)**
bacterium	bacteria
medium	media
alumna	alumnae
alumnus	alumni
fungus	fungi
datum	data
alga	algae
spaghetto	spaghetti
matrix	matrices
phenomenon	phenomena
attorney general	attorneys general
die	dice
index	indices, indexes
formula	formulae, formulas
brother	brothers, brethren
city-state	city-states

6. Notice from table 1.4.1 that:

   (a) Not all nouns ending in -*s* are plural (e.g. *news, physics, crisis*).
   (b) Sometimes the singular and plural forms of a word are the same.
   (c) Some nouns do not have singular forms.
   (d) Some nouns, such as those referring to qualities or academic subjects, do not have plural forms.
   (e) Some nouns have more than one acceptable plural form.

7. Some plurals indicate diversity. For example, a store can sell many "foods."

8. When forming the plurals of nouns that are hyphenated or written as several words, consult a dictionary to determine which component words to pluralize. Usually, the noun (or the most important noun, if there are several) is the only pluralized word. If none of the component words are themselves nouns, simply make the final word plural.

9. Use -'s to form the plurals of letters, numbers, and symbols, as well as the plurals of terms referring to themselves as terms. For example, there are two *of*'s, no *#*'s, no *9*'s, and 14 *e*'s in the previous sentence. Using -'s to form plurals is meant to avoid ambiguity (e.g. "*word*'s" versus "*words*"). If forming the plural without the apostrophe causes no confusion, and if a plural formed using -'s could be confused for a possessive word, feel free to omit the apostrophe.

1.4.2   Case: nominative, objective, or possessive

Case describes the function of a noun. English has three cases: nominative, objective, and possessive.

Table 1.4.2: Examples of case

Nominative	Objective	Possessive
we	us	our | ours
they	them	their | theirs
I	me	my | mine
who	whom	whose

Only certain pronouns (see section 1.4.5) change form when used in the objective case. With all other nouns, the nominative and objective forms are the same. Below, we present some guidelines for using case correctly. Several of our examples use some of the forms in table 1.4.2.

1. A verb's subject(s) should be nominative case.

Example 53. Subjects in nominative case

1. **They** have finally arrived.
2. **We** are ready to go.
3. **They** and **I** are ready.

2. Nouns that complement prepositions (see 1.3), transitive verbs, and verbals (see 1.5) based on transitive verbs should be objective case.

Example 54. Complements in objective case

1. Everyone **but** them participated.

   Remark. But functions as a preposition meaning *except.*

2. Everyone participated **but** them.

   Remark. Everyone participated but they is incorrect, since *but* is being used as a preposition. You cannot interpret the sentence as a shortened version of *everyone participated, but they did not*, since such a sentence would be illogical: if they did not participate, then *everyone participated* must be false.

3. We walked **beside** <u>them</u>.

4. We intended **to assist** <u>them</u>.

5. We **gave** <u>them</u> help.

6. We **assisted** <u>them</u>.

7. We **named** <u>them</u> <u>Chief Consultants</u>.

   Remark. *Them* and *Chief Consultants* complement the verb *named* and are thus objective.

8. An agreement exists **between** <u>you</u> and <u>me</u>.

   Remark. *Between you and I* is a common mistake. Both pronouns are objects of the preposition *between* and thus should be objective case.

9. The photographer took a picture **of** my <u>friend</u> and <u>me</u>.

10. The artist created a sculpture **depicting** my <u>friend</u> and <u>me</u>.

There is one notable exception to guideline 2: complements of the preposition *of* can be possessive case. Because *of* can express relationships other than possession, a possessive word can help clarify the preposition's meaning. *A photograph of them* and *a photograph of theirs* express different ideas. The latter phrase uses *of* to express membership in a group, and *theirs* is a possessive word that functions as a noun meaning *their photographs.* An equivalent statement would be *one of their photographs. A photograph of them* means *a photograph displaying them.*

Generally though, there is little point in using a double possessive such as *a friend of the professor's.* Say "a friend of the professor" or "the professor's friend" instead.

3. An infinitive that complements a transitive verb will sometimes itself have a subject. The subjects (sometimes called actors) of infinitives should be objective case, since they complement the same transitive verb the infinitive does.

Example 55. Subjects of infinitives

1. We want **them** to succeed.
2. We want **them** to surpass us.

4. Nouns associated by linking verbs (or verbals based on linking verbs) should be the same case.

Generally, linking verbs and their verbals associate something with a subject, so any nouns complementing them are usually nominative.

In speech, when following a linking verb with nominative case sounds awkward, you can ignore rule 4.

Example 56. Nouns associated by linking verbs are the same case.

1. The **person** in charge is **I**.
2. The **people** responsible are **they**.

Verbals based on linking verbs sometimes associate things with nouns in objective case. When they do, their complements should also be objective case.

Example 57. Nouns associated by verbals based on linking verbs are the same case.

1. We would not want **them** to be **us**.

   Remark. The complement of *to be* is linked to the subject of the infinitive, *them*. Therefore, the complement is objective case.

2. **We** would not want to be **they**.

   Remark. The complement of *to be* is linked to the subject of the sentence and is nominative case.

3. The administration believed the best **employees** to be **them**.

   Remark. The complement of *to be* is associated with a noun in objective case, *employees*. Therefore, the complement of *to be* should also be objective.

4. **Who** did **you** choose to be?

   Remark. *Who*, the complement of the infinitive *to be*, is associated with the subject *you*. Therefore, the nominative form *who* should be used. Mentally rewording the sentence to read "you did choose to be who" makes it easier to analyze.

5. When using *than* or *as* to make a comparison, mentally fill in missing words to determine case.

Example 58. Nouns in comparison

1. **We** ate more than **they**.
2. **They** are as experienced as **we**.
3. The supervisor observed **us** more than **them**.

The reasoning behind this rule is that you're not actually comparing nouns. For example, the sentence *I work more than you* is not making the nonsensical claim that "I" am more than "you" (whatever that means). Rather, how much "I work" is more than something else. Furthermore, the sentence *I work more than you* does not make any sense when interpreted as is, because the two elements of comparison are *I work* and *you*. The intended comparison is between how much "I work" and how much "you work."

When people say something like *I work more than you*, they are omitting part of the sentence. What they actually mean is *I work more than you work*.

In other words, the sentences in example 58 are actually abridged. The complete statements are:

- We ate more than they ate.
- They are as experienced as we are experienced.
- The supervisor observed us more than the supervisor observed them.

The case you use when comparing nouns indicates what is omitted and can affect the meaning of your statement. Consider the sentences in example 59.

Example 59. Meaning that depends on case

1. We like reading more than them.
2. We like reading more than they.

Remark. The first sentence actually means *we like reading more than we like them.* The second sentence actually means *we like reading more than they like reading.*

6. Appositives, which serve only to rename something, should be the same case as the nouns they refer to.

Example 60. Cases of appositives

1. Your guards — he, she, and I — will accompany you.
   Remark. He, she, and I renames the subject, and thus nominative case is appropriate.
2. We guards will accompany you.
3. You will be accompanied by guards — him, her, and me.
   Remark. Him, her, and me renames the object of a preposition, and thus objective case is appropriate.
4. You will be accompanied by guards — us.
5. The guards that you have selected, my friend and I, will accompany you.
   Remark. My friend and I renames *guards*, and thus nominative case is appropriate. *Friend* and *I* have nothing to do with complementing *selected*.

7. Use possessive case to show possession or association.

Example 61. Possessive case

1. the aircraft's passengers
2. Europe's landscape
3. the company's managers
4. the company's profits
5. my hat

With the exception of independent possessives (e.g. *mine, theirs*), possessive forms function as modifiers and cannot (1) serve as antecedents or (2) be in apposition to nouns.

Example 62. Proper possessive usage

1. Wrong: It's the professor's idea, who is extremely creative.

   Remark. Professor's is a modifier. It cannot be the antecedent of *who*.

2. Right: The idea came from the professor, who is extremely creative.

3. Wrong: It's the professor's idea, a Nobel laureate.

   Remark. The noun *laureate* cannot be in apposition to the modifier *professor's*.

4. Right: The idea came from the professor, a Nobel laureate.

5. Right: It was your friend's, the professor's, idea.

   Remark. A possessive word can be in apposition to a possessive word. The sentence is awkward, though.

6. Right: If you're out of ideas, try the professor's, which worked for me.

   Remark. Professor's now functions as a noun, so *which* can refer to it.

With nouns other than certain pronouns, forming the possessive is a simple matter: add an apostrophe to the end of the noun if it is plural and ends in -*s*; otherwise, add -*'s* to the end of the noun.

Example 63. Forming possessive words

1. child's

   Remark. belonging to one child

2. children's

   Remark. belonging to multiple children

3. plant's

   Remark. belonging to one plant

4. plants'

   Remark. belonging to multiple plants

5. Mars's

   Remark. belonging to Mars (e.g. *Mars's moons*)

6. brother-in-law's

   Remark. belonging to one brother-in-law

7. brothers-in-law's

   Remark. belonging to multiple brothers-in-law

When expressing several associations together, clearly specify whether entities own something jointly or independently and whether what they own is singular or plural.

Example 64. A vague association

The houses of both

Remark. The phrase could suggest that (1) two people jointly own several houses, (2) two people independently own several houses, or (3) each of two people owns one house.

Example 65. Expressing several associations together

1. Watson's and Crick's idea
   Remark. One idea belongs to both people.

2. Watson's idea and Crick's idea
   Remark. Each person possesses one idea, for a total of two ideas.

3. Watson's and Crick's ideas
   Remark. Multiple ideas are jointly owned. That is, both people possess each idea.

4. Watson's ideas and Crick's ideas
   Remark. There are two groups of multiple ideas. One belongs to Watson; the other belongs to Crick.

5. Watson's idea and Crick's ideas
   Remark. One idea belongs to Watson, and multiple ideas belong to Crick.

6. Watson and Crick's idea
   Remark. A person and an idea. The idea belongs to Crick.

7. Watson and Crick's ideas
   Remark. A person and several ideas. The ideas belong to Crick.

Unfortunately, the usages we suggest in example 65 are nonstandard, though they seem to us clearer than the current conventions. Most people will use the structure of sentence 6 to express the meaning we assign to sentence 1, and the structure of sentence 3 to express the meaning we assign to sentence 2. These conventions restrict your ability to express the meanings we assign to sentences 6 and 3.

You're better off avoiding these potentially confusing constructions altogether. How you express complex ownership isn't particularly important, as long as you clearly convey the nature of the ownership (i.e. joint or independent) and the nature of what is owned (i.e. singular or plural).

Example 66. Clearly expressing several associations

1. Watson and Crick came up with an idea. Their idea is about DNA.
2. Watson and Crick each came up with an idea. Watson's idea is based on Crick's idea.
3. Watson and Crick each came up with several ideas.
4. Watson and Crick came up with several ideas together.
5. The idea attributed to Watson and Crick is significant.

8. Carefully consider the role of a present participle.

The following two sentences look similar but have different meanings.

- *The people's cheering was disruptive.*
- *The people cheering were disruptive.*

In the first sentence, the cheering itself is disruptive. *Cheering* functions as a noun that *people's* modifies. In the second sentence, the people are disruptive, and *cheering* modifies *people*.

Think about what you're actually trying to say, then decide whether the present participle should modify or be modified. If you are using a present participle as a noun, and the activity described by the participle "belongs" to an entity, then you should use the possessive case to associate the participle with that entity. Some examples appear below.

Example 67. Participles as nouns being modified

1. Do you mind **their being** here?
2. They appreciated **my donating**.
3. I would be more comfortable with **our** both **going**.

   Remark. This statement is easier to justify than "I would be more comfortable with both of us going."

An easy test is to evaluate the meaning of the statement after eliminating the participle or the entity associated with it.

Example 68. Deciding between *them* and *their*

Original sentence: It was performed without them knowing.

Version 1: It was performed without them.

Version 2: It was performed without knowing.

Remark. Version 2 better preserves the meaning of the original sentence, so *them* should be possessive, and the sentence should read *it was performed without their knowing.*

When using the possessive case is logical but impractical, you can try to recast your statement.

Example 69.

Do you mind a person you don't recognize being here?

Remark. Though the "being here," not the person, is what you might mind, *person* cannot be possessive, because it is modified by the clause "(that) you don't recognize." The sentence can be reworded as "do you mind the presence of a person you don't recognize?"

Sometimes rewording is impractical, and you are better off not trying to convey the possession, even though expressing the possession would be logical.

Example 70.

There are no problems with students transferred from abroad maintaining their previous credits.

Remark. Maintaining is what there are no problems with, but "students transferred from abroad" cannot easily be made possessive. The sentence is acceptable as it is.

One more thing: in a construction such as "the work having been finished, we took a break," *having* is not a noun, so do not make *work* possessive.

9. The case of a noun is determined by the function the noun performs in its own clause (i.e. the clause containing the noun in the fewest words).

Example 71.

1. It brings good luck to <whoever possesses it>.

   Remark. Whoever is not the object of the preposition *to. Whoever* is the subject of the verb *possesses.* The bracketed clause "whoever possesses it" is the object of *to.* "Whoever possesses" is the smallest clause containing *whoever.*

2. Who shall I say is calling?

   Remark. Who is the subject of the verb *is,* not the object of the verb *say.* "Who is calling" is the object of *say.* The grammatical relationships are easier to see with some mental rearranging: "I shall say who is calling?"

3. The police will arrest <whoever breaks the law>.

4. The police will arrest him <who breaks the law>.

5. <It was they><I was referring to>.

   Remark. "I was referring to" is a clause modifying *they.* The object of the preposition *to* is implied: the complete statement is "that I was referring to." *They* should be nominative because it is linked to the subject *it,* a nominative word. *They* is not the object of the preposition *to.*

6. Please notify whoever that is your friend is talking to.

   Remark. The grammar of the sentence is easier to understand if we identify the clauses, rearrange the words, and fill in an implied relative pronoun: "Please notify <that is whoever>< (that) your friend is talking to>." The clause "that is whoever" is the object of *notify.* The clause "(that) your friend is talking to" modifies *whoever,* which is linked to a subject and is thus nominative. "Please notify whomever your friend is talking to" is better.

7. I have a friend who I am sure can help you.

   Remark. Who is the subject of *can help.*

8. I do not know <whom you confused me for>.

   Remark. The clause "whom you confused me for" is the object of *do know. Whom* is the object of the preposition *for.*

9. They select <whomever they want>.

   Remark. Whomever is the object of *want.* The clause "whomever they want" is the object of *select.*

1.4.3   Person: first, second, or third

1. First person nouns indicate those speaking or writing (e.g. *I, myself, we, us*).

2. Second person nouns indicate those being addressed (e.g. *you, yourself*).

3. Third person nouns indicate third parties (e.g. *he, she, it, they, himself, herself, itself, themselves*).

1.4.4   Gender: masculine, feminine, common, or neuter

1. Nouns that refer only to males are **masculine** (e.g. *father*).

2. Nouns that refer only to females are **feminine** (e.g. *mother*).

3. Nouns of **common** gender can refer to males and females (e.g. *parent*).

4. Most English nouns are **neuter** — that is, they are not masculine, feminine, or common (e.g. *electricity, dirt, fire*).

Once you establish an entity's gender, refer to it consistently. For example, you can refer to a bird with *he, she,* or *it,* but don't call the bird *he* in one sentence and *it* (or *she,* for that matter) in another sentence. Generally, people make this sort of mistake only when dealing with nonhuman entities; it's easy to forget whether a pet, an android, a centaur, or the Balrog is a *he* or an *it.*

Shifts in gender are permissible if there is a sensible reason for them. If you discuss birds in general using *it* and then begin specifically discussing male birds, switching to *he* in that part of the discussion is reasonable. Consider context when determining gender, and make sure any shifts do not confuse the reader.

1.4.5   Pronouns

Pronouns can stand in for other nouns (including other pronouns). The table below contains examples of six types of pronouns.

Table 1.4.3: Types of pronouns

Pronoun type	Examples
Personal	I, we, you, he, she, it, they, me, us, him, her, them, my, mine, your, yours, his, her, hers, its
Demonstrative	this, that, these, those
Interrogative	who(ever), whom(ever), whose(ver), which(ever), what(ever), where, when
Indefinite	all, another, any, anybody, anyone, anything, both, each, either, enough, everybody, everyone, everything, few, less, many, most, neither, no one, nobody, none, nothing, one, ones, other, others, plenty, several, some, somebody, someone, something
Relative	who(ever), whom(ever), whose(ver), which(ever), what(ever), where, when, that
Reflexive	myself, ourselves, yourself, yourselves, himself, herself, itself, oneself, themselves

Some important information about pronouns:

1. An **antecedent** is an expression a pronoun refers to.

2. A pronoun is not required to have an antecedent. Indefinite pronouns, for example, by nature do not refer to anything specific.

3. Antecedents are not required to go before the pronouns that refer to them.

4. A pronoun and its antecedent must agree in person, number, and gender. For more information about this rule, see 1.11.

5. Except for **independent possessives** (e.g. *mine, yours, ours, theirs*), which are considered nouns, a possessive pronoun works as a modifier, just as most possessive nouns do. Not all pronouns have a possessive form.

6. Some terms that function as pronouns can function as modifiers also.

7. Case, person, number, and gender are the four variables that can affect the form of a pronoun, though not every variable affects every type of pronoun. For example, demonstrative pronouns change form based on number only, while reflexive pronouns change based on gender, person, and number. All four variables affect personal pronouns.

Below, we discuss each type of pronoun in more detail. We also show whatever effect case, person, number, and gender may have on form.

1.4.5.1 Singular personal pronouns

Table 1.4.4: Singular personal pronouns

	Nominative	Objective	Possessive
First person	I	me	my | mine
Second person	you	you	your | yours
Third person	he (masculine)	him (masculine)	his (masculine)
	she (feminine)	her (feminine)	her | hers (feminine)
	it (neuter)	it (neuter)	its (neuter)

- *His* and *its* may function as ordinary possessives (e.g. *its color*) or independent ones (e.g. *his is better*).
- Always capitalize the pronoun *I*.

1.4.5.2 Plural personal pronouns

Table 1.4.5: Plural personal pronouns

	Nominative	Objective	Possessive
First person	we	us	our | ours
Second person	you	you	your | yours
Third person	they	them	their | theirs

1.4.5.3 Reflexive (intensive) pronouns

Table 1.4.6: Reflexive pronouns

	Singular	Plural
First person	myself	ourselves
Second person	yourself	yourselves
Third person	himself (masculine)	themselves
	herself (feminine)	
	itself (neuter)	
	oneself	

Unless they are used for emphasis, reflexive pronouns should indicate the entity responsible for the action or state they complement. Usually, reflexive pronouns refer to the subject of their own clause.

When used for emphasis, a reflexive pronoun may refer to any noun, though.

Example 72.

1. Though the players tried to be careful, they injured themselves.
   Remark. Themselves refers to *they*, the subject of "they injured themselves."

2. We met the founders themselves.
   Remark. Themselves serves to emphasize. It refers to *founders* rather than to the subject, *we*.

3. I myself will participate.
   Remark. Myself emphasizes *I*, the subject of the clause.

4. We built this ourselves.
   Remark. Ourselves is used for emphasis and refers to the subject of the clause.

5. Control yourself.
   Remark. Yourself refers to the implicit subject of the command, *you*.

6. Strengthening oneself can be challenging.
   Remark. Oneself refers to the one performing the strengthening.

Do not use reflexive pronouns as personal pronouns (or vice versa).

Example 73.

Wrong: A person like yourself would be perfect.

Right: A person like you would be perfect.

Wrong: He's stronger than myself.

Right: He's stronger than I am.

1.4.5.4 Demonstrative pronouns

Table 1.4.7: Demonstrative pronouns

Singular	Plural
this	these
that	those

1. *This, that, these,* and *those* can be modifiers. As modifiers, they must agree in number with whatever they are describing. Don't be fooled by prepositional phrases, especially when dealing with words such as *kind, sort,* and *type*.

Example 74.

Wrong: I love these kind of clothes.
Remark. These modifies *kind,* not *clothes.*

Wrong: I love this kinds of clothes.

Right: I love this kind of clothes.

Right: I love these kinds of clothes.

Right: I love this kind of clothing.

Right: I love these kinds of clothing.

2. *This* and *these* refer to things that are near the speaker.
3. *That* and *those* refer to things that are farther away from the speaker.

1.4.5.5 Relative pronouns

Table 1.4.8: Relative pronouns

Nominative	Objective	Possessive
who	whom	whose
whoever	whomever	whosever

1. Aside from *who* and *whoever*, which change form based on case only, relative pronouns are unaffected by case, person, number, and gender.
2. The relative pronoun *that* can be singular or plural, but the demonstrative pronoun *that* is strictly singular.
3. *Which(ever)* and *what(ever)* are also modifiers.
4. Traditionally, the various forms of *who* must refer to entities with human characteristics. However, *whose* and *whosever* can refer to things as well (e.g. *a company whose assets are valuable, a word whose meaning is clear*).
5. The antecedents of *which(ever)* or *what(ever)* should never be people. However, the terms can be used with people in other situations (e.g. *which person, which of the students, whichever of you*).
6. *That* can be used with people or things.
7. *That* makes a relative clause **restrictive**. Restrictive relative clauses limit or define what they are referring to. In contrast, *which* and *who* are used in **nonrestrictive** clauses, which merely provide extra information.

Example 75. *Which* and *that*

Restrictive: words **that begin with the letter** *m*
Remark. The clause identifies a particular group of words.

Nonrestrictive: computers, **which require energy to function**
Remark. The clause serves to provide information rather than restrict discussion to a certain group.

8. *Which* and *who* can be used in restrictive clauses, though we recommend trying to use *that* instead. Sometimes, however, restrictively using *who* or *which* is unavoidable (e.g. *that which challenges you makes you stronger*). Distinguishing between *that* and *which* is more useful in speech than it is in writing, since commas set off nonrestrictive relative clauses but not restrictive ones.

9. You can often omit a relative pronoun functioning as an object in a restrictive clause (e.g. *here is the article (that) I was talking about*). If you are unsure about the acceptability of a particular omission, supply the pronoun to be on the safe side.

10. *Whosoever*, *whomsoever*, and *whosesoever* are variants of *whoever*, *whomever*, and *whosever*, respectively. *Whatsoever* is used almost exclusively as an adverb meaning "at all" (e.g. *none whatsoever*). People no longer use *whatsoever* to mean *whatever*.

11. *Whom(ever)* may be on its way out of the language. It is infrequently used in speech, but you should continue to use it in your writing for now.

1.4.5.6 Indefinite pronouns

Table 1.4.9: Indefinite pronouns

Singular	another, anybody, anyone, anything, each, either, enough, everybody, everyone, everything, less, little, much, neither, nobody, no one, nothing, other, one, somebody, someone, something
Plural	both, few, many, ones, others, several
Either	all, any, most, none, some

1. The pronouns in the third row of table 1.4.9 change number depending on what they refer to. If they refer to something thought of as a whole, they are singular. Otherwise, they are plural.

Example 76.

1. **Most** of the **people are** going.

   Remark. People are considered individually, so *most* is plural, and the appropriate verb is *are*.

2. **Some** of the **water has** spilled.

   Remark. Water is considered a whole, so *some* is singular, and the appropriate verb is *has*.

2. *None* can be singular if used to mean "no individual."

Example 77.

None of us **is** capable of accomplishing this alone.

3. Many indefinite pronouns (e.g. *another, each, either, enough, less, little, much, neither, other, one, both, few, many, several, all, any, most, none, some*) may also function as modifiers.

4. *One* refers to a person in general (e.g. *one must be careful*) or to some previously mentioned or easily identified thing (e.g. *that is the one I wanted*). Using *you* to refer to a person in general is much more common, because *one* sounds overly formal to many. Don't shift unnecessarily when using *one*.

Example 78. Unnecessary shifts

Awkward: **One** should proofread **his** work.

Awkward: **One** should proofread **your** work.

Better: **One** should proofread **one's** work.

5. Generally, indefinite pronouns that specifically refer to people can be made possessive by adding -'s (e.g. *anybody's, anyone's, everybody's, everyone's, one's, nobody's, no one's, somebody's, someone's*). However, many of the indefinite pronouns simply do not have a possessive form (e.g. *less's* make no sense).

6. Traditionally, a masculine pronoun is used if the gender of an antecedent is unknown. Many people consider this usage impolite, however.

Example 79. Gender agreement

1. Every **woman** should proofread **her** work.
   Remark. feminine antecedent + feminine pronoun

2. Every **man** should proofread **his** work.
   Remark. masculine antecedent + masculine pronoun

3. Every **writer** should proofread **his** work.
   Remark. antecedent of unknown gender + male pronoun

4. Every **person** should proofread **his** work.
   Remark. antecedent of unknown gender + male pronoun

5. Every **employee** should proofread **his** work.
   Remark. antecedent of unknown gender + male pronoun

There are several ways to avoid the potentially impolite usage in sentences 3 through 5 of example 79:

1. *Everyone should proofread his or her work.*
2. *Everyone should proofread his/her work.*
3. *Everyone should proofread.*
4. *People should proofread their work.*
5. *You should proofread your work.*

Using "his/her" or "his or her" can become clumsy, especially when such terms must be repeated many times in a sentence or paragraph. Try recasting your statement to eliminate any troublesome pronouns (i.e. alternative 3). If elimination is not possible, you can try using plural pronouns (i.e. alternative 4) or second person pronouns (i.e. alternative 5) to avoid specifying gender.

In some situations, you may have to write something awkward or leave out one gender.

1.5 Verbals

Though derived from verbs, verbals actually function as other parts of speech. Verbals may have complements.

A **gerund** is a participle used as a noun.

Example 80. Gerunds

1. **Photographing** nature is my favorite activity.
2. **Having survived** illness makes me grateful.

Participles can also function as modifiers.

Example 81. Participles as modifiers

1. a **growing** person
2. a fully **grown** person

An **infinitive** is the base form of a verb used as a noun or a modifier. An infinitive often begins with *to*.

Example 82. Infinitives

1. I want **to leave**.
   Remark. The infinitive complements *want*.

2. You would have me **think** of you as a criminal?
   Remark. The infinitive *think* complements the verb *have*.

3. We made them **reconsider** the plan.
   Remark. The infinitive *reconsider* complements the verb *made*. *Plan* complements *reconsider*.

4. **To explore** other planets is my dream.
   Remark. *To explore other planets* is the subject.

5. I work **to help** others.
   Remark. *To help others* modifies *work*.

6. Now is the time **to act**.
   Remark. The infinitive *to act* modifies *time*.

Sometimes, something will separate the *to* from the verb form, resulting in a **split infinitive** (e.g. *to loudly speak*). Split an infinitive if doing so improves the clarity or fluidity of your writing, but avoid senselessly splitting infinitives.

Using an adverb to separate an auxiliary from a main verb does not qualify as splitting an infinitive. For example, "it seems to have mysteriously vanished" does not contain a split infinitive.

Example 83. Splitting infinitives

1. You really have **to learn** this.

   Remark. The sentence means "learning this is important." "You have **to** really **learn** this" means "you must learn this thoroughly." Splitting the infinitive in this case actually changes the meaning of the sentence.

2. He wanted **to strike** the ball suddenly.

   Remark. *Suddenly* could modify either *wanted* or *strike.* To be clear, write "he suddenly wanted to strike the ball" or "he wanted to suddenly strike the ball," depending on your intended meaning. Splitting the infinitive in this case is a matter of clarity.

3. **To** carefully, deliberately, repeatedly — even without rest — **practice.**

   Remark. Too much separates *to* from *practice.* "To practice carefully, deliberately, repeatedly — even without rest" sounds better anyway. Splitting the infinitive in this case is a bad idea.

Verbals also exhibit voice and time.

Table 1.5.1: Participles by voice and time

Participles	Active	Passive
Non-past	choosing	being chosen
Past	having chosen	chosen, having been chosen

Table 1.5.2: Infinitives by voice and time

Infinitives	Active	Passive
Non-past	to choose	to be chosen
Past	to have chosen	to have been chosen

Example 84.

1. **Being chosen** was a surprise.
2. **Having been chosen**, I walked to the front.
3. **Chosen**, I walked to the front.
4. **To be chosen** is a great honor.
5. **To have been chosen** is a great honor.

A verbal expresses time in relation to the time of a verb in the same sentence. A present verbal occurs at the same time as the verb (whenever that might be); a past verbal occurs before. If a sentence contains verbs referring to different times, make clear which verbs a verbal associates with.

Example 85.

1. **Inspired** by the setting sun, I **wrote** a poem.
   Remark. The inspiration occurred before the writing; both are past events.

2. **Being chased** by a wild animal, I **ran** as fast as I could.
   Remark. The chasing and the running occurred at the same time in the past.

3. **Having chosen** one of the options, I **hope** for the best.
   Remark. The choosing occurs before the hoping; the hoping occurs in the present.

4. **Choosing** one of the options, I **hope** for the best.
   Remark. The choosing and the hoping occur at the same time in the present.

5. **Having chosen** one of the options, I **will hope** for the best.
   Remark. The choosing occurs before the hoping; the hoping occurs in the future.

6. **Choosing** one of the options, I **will hope** for the best.
   Remark. The choosing and the hoping occur at the same time in the future.

Remember, present verbals convey simultaneity. Don't use them to express sequences of events.

Example 86.

Wrong: Hanging up my coat, I washed my hands.
Remark. Did I hang up my coat while washing my hands? Probably not.

Right: I hung up my coat and then washed my hands.

1.6 Interjections

Interjections convey emotions and do not have any grammatical relationships to other words. Interjections do not qualify as sentences.

Use an exclamation mark with a strong emotion; use a comma with a mild emotion.

Example 87. Interjections

1. **Wow! Hey!**
2. **Ow!** That hurt.
3. **Okay**, we can go now.

4. **Well**, what do you think?

5. **Oh**, I didn't see you there.

1.7 Conjunctions

Conjunctions connect grammatical elements.

Example 88. Notice how the conjunctions connect the bracketed elements.

1. Nouns: <determination>, <strength>, **or** <honor>
2. Clauses: <We left>, **since** <we finished>. **Although** <the trip was short>, <it was enjoyable>.
3. Verbs: **both** <slice> **and** <dice>
4. Adjectives: **not only** <simple> **but also** <effective>
5. Prefixes: <pre-> **and** <post-> treatment health
6. Phrases

   (a) Prepositional phrases: <out of the frying pan> **and** <into the fire>
   (b) Verb + complement: I <tried everything > **and** <wrote down the results>.

There are three types of conjunctions. Table 1.7.1 contains examples of each kind.

Table 1.7.1: Types of conjunctions

Type	Examples
Subordinating	after, although, as, as if, as long as, as soon as, as though, because, before, even though, how, if, in order that, inasmuch as, provided (that), since, so, so that, than, that, till, unless, until, when(ever), where(ver), whereas, while, why, even if, if only, except that, in case, ever since, just as
Coordinating	and, but, or, nor, for, yet
Correlative	either...or, neither...nor, both...and, not only...but also, whether...or, just as...so, not...but

Some notes about conjunctions:

1. Some words that serve as conjunctions can serve as other parts of speech, such as adverbs or prepositions.
2. *Thus, then, however, consequently, therefore, also, moreover, besides, indeed,* and *nevertheless* are adverbs, not conjunctions.
3. *Either* and *neither* can introduce more than two alternatives (e.g. *either north, east, or south*).
4. When trying to use a correlative conjunction, be sure to use the second half of it correctly.

   (a) Take care to include *also* (or some synonym) in constructions with *not only...but also.*
   (b) *Neither* is traditionally followed by *nor*, not *or*.

Example 89. Using both parts of a correlative conjunction

Wrong: **Not only** is the treatment safe, it is effective.

Wrong: **Not only** is the treatment safe, but it is effective.

Right: **Not only** is the treatment safe, **but** it is **also** effective.

Right: **Not only** is the treatment safe, **but** it is effective **as well**.

Right: **Not only** is the treatment safe, **but** it is effective **too**.

Right: **Not only** is the treatment safe — it is **also** effective.
Remark. A dash can replace *but* in this case.

Uncommon: Such actions are **neither** moral **or** legal.

Traditional: Such actions are **neither** moral **nor** legal.

5. Try to connect only elements that serve the same grammatical function. Make the connected elements as closely parallel as possible (i.e. structure the elements similarly).

Example 90.

1. Awkward: It is <portable>, <efficient>, and <it never fails>.
   Remark. Two adjectives are connected with a clause.

2. Better: <It is <portable> and <efficient> >, and <it never fails>.
   Remark. The first conjunction connects two adjectives; the second conjunction connects two clauses.

3. Better: It is <portable>, <efficient>, and <reliable>.
   Remark. The conjunction connects three adjectives.

4. Awkward: They are <skilled> and <athletes>.

5. Better: They are <skilled> and <athletic>.

The same principle applies to correlative conjunctions.

Example 91.

Awkward: I either <want to be a dancer> or <a singer>.

Better: I want to be either <a dancer> or <a singer>.

Awkward: I either <want to see a movie> or <read a book>.

Better: I want either <to see a movie> or <to read a book>.

Awkward: We neither <require food> nor <rest>.

Better: We require neither <food> nor <rest>.

Awkward: We not only <received food> but also <water>.

Better: We received not only <food> but also <water>.

6. *Not only...but also* logically expresses addition rather than negation, despite the presence of the word *not*. Don't confuse *not only...but also* with the correlative conjunction *not...but*, which expresses replacement.

Example 92.

1. We required not only <food> but also <water>.

   Remark. That is, we required "food and water" or "food in addition to water."

2. We required not <food> but <water>.

   Remark. We required water instead of food.

3. It was not <only a discovery> but <a revolutionary one>.

   Remark. Only is part of the elements connected rather than part of the correlative conjunction, so *also* is omitted despite the presence of *not only*. "It was not a minor discovery but a revolutionary one" is better.

1.8 Phrases

1. Think of a phrase as a group of words acting as a unit.
2. Phrases are often based on verbals, nouns, or prepositions. Such phrases include the verbal, noun, or preposition and can include anything that modifies, conjoins, or complements something else that belongs in the phrase.
3. Phrases can act as nouns or modifiers.

Example 93 illustrates some common types of phrases.

Example 93. Phrases

<Carefully finishing <my <partially built> fusion reactor> <before next week> > is necessary <to solve the world's energy problems>.

Comments on example 93:

- "Carefully finishing my partially built fusion reactor before next week" is a gerund phrase consisting of a gerund (*finishing*), the gerund's object (*reactor*), the gerund's modifiers (*carefully, before next week*), the gerund's object's modifiers (*my, built, fusion*), and the modifier of one of the object's modifiers (*partially*). This gerund phrase is the complete subject of *is*, the verb of the sentence.
- "Partially built" is a participle phrase consisting of a past participle (*built*) and the participle's modifier (*partially*). The phrase modifies the noun *reactor*.

- "My partially built fusion reactor" is a noun phrase that consists of a noun (*reactor*), its modifiers (*my, fusion, built*), and the modifier of one of its modifiers (*partially*).

- "To solve the world's energy problems" is an infinitive phrase consisting of an infinitive (*to solve*), the infinitive's object (*problems*), and the object's modifiers (*the, world's, energy*). This infinitive phrase modifies the adjective *necessary*.

- "Before next week" is a prepositional phrase consisting of a preposition (*before*), the preposition's object (*week*), and the object's modifier (*next*). This prepositional phrase modifies the gerund *finishing*.

1.9 Clauses

Like phrases, clauses are word groups and can act as nouns or modifiers. Unlike phrases, clauses must contain at least a subject and a corresponding verb. Clauses may contain more than one subject, and they may also contain more than one verb.

Every element in a clause must serve some grammatical purpose in it. For example:

- a subject of the clause
- a verb that corresponds to a subject of the clause
- anything that modifies or complements part of the clause
- anything in apposition to part of the clause
- anything that conjoins parts of the clause

Example 94. Clauses

After <he considered <what was best> >, my friend, <who recently moved>, purchased a car <that has advanced safety features>.

The following outline contains information about each clause that we identified in example 94.

- *what was best*

    - Subject: *what*
    - Verb: *was*
    - Function: object of the verb *considered*

- *who recently moved*

    - Subject: *who*
    - Verb: *moved*
    - Function: modifies *friend*

- *that has advanced safety features*

    - Subject: *that*
    - Verb: *has*
    - Function: modifies *car*

- *he considered what was best*

    - Subject: *he*
    - Verb: *considered*
    - Function: combines with *after* to modify *purchased*

Notice that nonrestrictive clauses such as "who recently moved" are marked off by commas. Restrictive clauses such as "that has advanced safety features" are not.

Example 94 contains many clauses, but it is actually just one sentence.

1.10 Sentences

In English, a written sentence should:

1. Begin with a capital letter.
2. Contain at least one clause.
3. Combine clauses appropriately (see 1.10.1).
4. End with appropriate terminal punctuation (see 1.10.2).

Furthermore, every element of the sentence should belong to a clause, serve to join elements of the sentence together, or belong to an interruption such as an interjection, a direct address, or a parenthetical expression.

Example 95. Invalid sentences

1. Because we arrived early.
   Remark. The conjunction *because* serves no purpose, as there is only one clause.

2. The blue sky.
   Remark. The statement does not contain at least one clause.

Sentences 1 and 2 of example 95 are known as **fragments**.

1.10.1 Properly joining clauses into a sentence

1. Place a comma and a conjunction between two clauses. If you're connecting many short clauses with the same conjunction, you can omit all but the final conjunction (e.g. *the flight was delayed, the food was awful, and the movie was full of clichés*).
2. Place a comma after a clause introduced by a subordinating conjunction.
3. Use a relative pronoun. Commas should separate inessential (i.e. nonrestrictive) clauses from the rest of the sentence.
4. Place a colon or semicolon between two clauses.
5. Use parentheses or dashes.

Table 1.10.1 illustrates the various methods for properly connecting clauses. The examples are adaptations of a quotation attributed to Bertrand Russell.

Table 1.10.1: Ways to join clauses

Connection method	Example(s)
Conjunction	Many people would sooner die than think, and in fact, they do so. Since many people would sooner die than think, they do so. Not only would people rather die than think, but they also do so.
Relative pronoun	People that would sooner die than think in fact do so. People, who would sooner die than think, in fact do so.
Semicolon	Many people would sooner die than think; in fact, they do so.
Colon	Many people would sooner die than think: in fact, they do so.

Dash	Many people would sooner die than think — in fact, they do so.
	Many people would — in fact, they do so — sooner die than think.
Parentheses	Many people would sooner die than think (in fact, they do so).
	Many people would (in fact, they do so) sooner die than think.

The method used to join two clauses should reflect how the content of one clause relates to the content of the other.

1. Use a conjunction that correctly describes the relationship between two clauses. For example:

    (a) Use **because** to show a cause-effect relationship.
    (b) Use **but**, **yet**, **whereas**, or **although** to combine contrasting ideas.
    (c) Use **and** to continue an idea.

2. Use a semicolon only if two closely related clauses could convey the same meaning as separate sentences.

3. Use a colon for a dramatic introduction or to show a causal relationship.

4. Use a dash to signal an afterthought or some other abrupt change in thought.

5. Use parentheses to enclose a qualifying, elaborative, or explanatory interruption.

Combining clauses without proper punctuation can result in an error call a **run-on sentence**. You can correct a run-on sentence by using a semicolon, a period, or a conjunction.

Example 96. Run-on sentences

1. We attended the meeting it was interesting.
2. We attended the meeting, it was interesting.

Ways to correct the flawed sentences in example 96 include:

- *We attended the meeting; it was interesting.*
- *We attended the meeting. It was interesting.*
- *We attended the meeting, and it was interesting.*
- *We attended the meeting, which was interesting.*

A **simple sentence**, also known as an **independent clause**, cannot be divided into multiple clauses.

1.10.2   Terminal punctuation

Terminal punctuation depends on the function of the sentence.

1. A **declarative** sentence makes a statement and ends with a period. For example, the previous sentence is declarative, and so is this one.

2. An **interrogative** sentence asks a question and ends with a question mark.

Example 97. Interrogative sentences

1. Who am I?
2. Why do we exist?
3. How do you know what is true?

3. An **imperative** sentence states a request or a command and ends with a period.

Example 98. Imperative sentences

1. Go.
2. Prepare yourself.
3. Be careful.

4. If you wish to express a strong emotion, use an exclamation mark instead of a period. Don't put an exclamation mark with a question mark (!?, ?!, ?!?, etc.) in formal writing.

Example 99. Exclamation

1. It's finally here!
2. What is that?!
3. Stop that!

5. Use exclamation marks sparingly, since overusing them will annoy readers.

Example 100. Excessive use of exclamation marks

Hardwood floors! Great location!!! State-of-the-art kitchen is A+++++++!!!!!

One more note about sentences: In formal work (e.g. school assignments, business proposals, research publications), you should write in complete sentences. That is, every word used to express your ideas should belong to a sentence. Complete sentences are neither necessary nor sufficient for clear and meaningful writing, but they help encourage it.

1.11   Agreement

1. Subjects and their corresponding verbs must agree in person and number. Keep in mind that subjects may appear long after their verbs.

2. Some verb forms never change and thus can agree with any subject.

3. A pronoun and its antecedent must agree in person, number, and gender. Agreement in gender is a concern only when using a personal or reflexive pronoun that is third person singular.

Example 101. Pronoun-antecedent agreement

1. Though **they** searched everywhere, the **guards** found nothing.

   Remark. *Guards* is the antecedent of *they*. Both *guards* and *they* are third person and plural. Because *guards* is plural, agreement in gender does not have to be considered.

2. Did you see the **woman** that just walked by? **She** waved at us.

   Remark. *Woman* is the antecedent of *she*. Both *woman* and *she* are singular, third person, and feminine.

4. A verb does not have to agree with its complements, though a complement may indicate whether you should consider a numerically ambiguous subject singular or plural.

Example 102.

1. The fireworks are a diversion.

   Remark. The verb *are* agrees with its plural subject, *fireworks*. *Are* does not have to agree with its singular complement, *diversion*.

2. It is examples that will help you understand.

   Remark. *Is* agrees with *it*, a singular subject. *Is* does not agree with *examples*, a plural complement.

5. A relative pronoun takes on the person, number, and gender of its antecedent.

Example 103.

1. Earth is one of the many <u>planets that</u> **have** a moon.

   Remark. *That* refers to *planets* and is thus plural, so *have* is the appropriate verb form.

2. Is Earth the only <u>one of the planets that</u> **has** intelligent life?

   Remark. *That* refers to *one* and is thus singular, so *has* is the appropriate verb form.

3. <u>I, who</u> **speak** to you, am he.

   Remark. *Who* refers to *I*, so *speak* is the appropriate form.

4. I am <u>he who</u> **speaks** to you.

   Remark. *Who* refers to *he*, so *speaks* is the appropriate form.

5. You are the <u>one that</u> is too strict with **himself**.

   Remark. Saying "too strict with yourself" is incorrect in this case. *Himself* refers to *that*, and the antecedent of *that* is *one*, which is third person. *Yourself* is a second person pronoun.

6. This is a <u>person</u> <u>that</u> submitted **his or her** application early.

   Remark. Person is singular, so *that* is singular. Therefore, any pronoun referring to *that* should also be singular. *Their application* would be incorrect.

7. I spoke with my <u>sister</u>, <u>who</u> submitted **her** application early.

   Remark. Who is feminine because it refers to *sister*. Pronouns that refer to *who* must therefore also be feminine.

Following this rule can cause awkwardness in more complicated sentences. For instance, what is the appropriate verb to use in example 104?

Example 104. Which verb in brackets should you choose?

It is I that [is | am] held responsible.

The antecedent of *that* determines the appropriate verb in this case. Technically, the antecedent is *it* (i.e. the "filler" subject), and so the verb should be *is*. However, many argue that *I* is the antecedent and that *am* is the appropriate verb. We recommend using the filler subject as the antecedent unless doing so makes the sentence sound awkward.

Example 105.

1. It is not I that is held responsible.

   Remark. Making *that* correspond to the filler subject usually sounds better when the complement involves negation.

2. It is we that is held responsible.

   Remark. The differences in person and number cause the sentence to sound strange. "It is we that are held responsible" sounds better.

In short, use whatever verb sounds best. Better yet, avoid complicated expressions such as "it is I and not you that is held responsible." Say something like "I am held responsible; you're not."

Another troublesome pronoun is *what*, which can be either singular or plural. You can choose either verb in example 106, depending on what you think *what* refers to.

Example 106. Either verb in brackets is acceptable.

New ideas are what [is | are] helpful.

What *what* represents is sometimes unclear, so we recommend examining other parts of the sentence for clues.

Example 107. Other troublesome situations involving *what*

1. What puzzles us is the unusual delays.

   Remark. What can represent something singular despite the presence of a plural complement. Clauses such as "what puzzles us" are technically singular, so *is* is the appropriate verb. "What puzzle us are the unusual delays" is also arguable, though it is more difficult to justify.

2. What are called flaws are often just quirks.

   Remark. Regarding the clause "what are called flaws" as singular leads to the strange sentence "what are called flaws is often just quirks." Go ahead and treat a clause as plural if you think it clearly represents a plural idea.

6. When nouns are joined by *or, nor,* or *not only...but also,* determine agreement using whichever noun is closest to the verb or pronoun you are trying to make agree. Often, using distance to determine agreement makes for an awkward sentence, and you are better off rephrasing.

Example 108.

1. Either Mars or its **moons have** intelligent life.
2. Either its moons or **Mars has** intelligent life.

Remark. You use *has* or *have* based on whether *moons* or *Mars* is closer to the verb.

3. Neither my coworkers nor my **brother** brought **his** equipment.
4. Neither my brother nor my **coworkers** brought **their** equipment.
5. Neither my brother nor my **sister** brought **her** equipment.
6. Neither my sister nor my **brother** brought **his** equipment.
7. Only one or **two** of them **are** authentic.
8. Either you or **I am** capable of operating the machinery.
9. Neither I nor **you are** capable of operating the machinery.

Remark. As expected, many of these example sentences are awkward. When following the rules results in clumsiness, rephrase:

- Either Mars has intelligent life, or its moons do.
- My coworkers did not bring their equipment. My brother did not bring his, either.
- Neither of us is capable of operating the machinery.

Example 109.

1. Not only the coach but also the **players were** interviewed.

2. Not only the players but also the **coach was** interviewed.
3. Not only **was** the **coach** interviewed, but also the players.
4. Not only **were** the **players** interviewed, but also the coach.

If you are trying to match a multi-word verb with nouns connected by *or*, *nor*, or *not only...but also*, make the verb agree with whichever noun is closer to the part of the verb that changes based on number.

Example 110.

1. **Does** either **Mars** or its moons **have** intelligent life?
2. **Do** either its **moons** or Mars **have** intelligent life?
3. **Does** neither **Mars** nor its moons **have** intelligent life?
4. **Do** neither its **moons** nor Mars **have** intelligent life?

Remark. Use *do* or *does* based on whether *Mars* or *moons* is closer to the auxiliary, since the auxiliary is the part of the verb that changes. *Have* never changes here.

7. If a negative subject (i.e. a subject expressing the absence rather than the presence of something) is compounded with a positive one, the positive one determines agreement. Note that subjects joined by "not only...but also" are logically positive despite the presence of the negative word *not*.

Example 111.

1. The **players** and not the coach **were** interviewed.
2. The **coach** and not the players **was** interviewed.
3. **I** and not you **am** invisible.
4. **You** and not I **are** invisible.

You can reposition the negative subject if you think it is awkwardly placed. Doing so also makes determining proper agreement easier.

Example 112.

1. The players were interviewed, not the coach.
2. The coach was interviewed, not the players.

1.11.1 Guidelines for identifying subjects and verbs

1. Ignore verbals when attempting to identify verbs. Verbals act as nouns or modifiers — never as verbs.

Example 113. The verb of each example sentence is bold.

1. To prove my point, I **showed** several photographs.

   Remark. To prove my point is an infinitive phrase that modifies the verb *showed.*

2. Having rested, I **was prepared** for the next match.

   Remark. Having rested is a participle that modifies the subject *I.*

3. **Does** resting **improve** mental function?

   Remark. Resting, a present participle used as a noun, is the subject of the sentence.

4. We **had** them recall as many details as possible.

   Remark. Recall is an infinitive functioning as a noun.

5. We **were asked** to recall as many details as possible.

   Remark. To recall is an infinitive functioning as a noun.

2. After you identify a verb, ask yourself who or what is performing the action the verb expresses. The answer to this question will be the verb's subject.

Example 114. Identifying subjects

1. **I** washed my hands.

   Remark. Who or what **washed**? **I** washed, so *I* is the subject.

2. **It** was time to go.

   Remark. Who or what **was**? **It** was, so *it* is the subject.

3. Around the world flew the **airplane**.

   Remark. Who or what flew? The **airplane** flew, so *airplane* is the subject.

4. Is **that** Mars?

   Remark. Who or what **is**? **That** is, so *that* is the subject.

5. What does that **person** want?

   Remark. Who or what **does want**? The **person** does want, so *person* is the subject.

6. Try again.

   Remark. Who or what should **try**? **You** should try, so *you* is the (understood) subject.

7. The entire **area** has been searched by the police.

   Remark. Who or what **has been searched**? The **area** has been searched, so *area* is the subject.

3. Ignore complements when trying to identify a subject.

Example 115.

1. A **variety** of options is available.

   Remark. Variety is the subject; *is* is the verb. *Options* is the object of the preposition *of.* "Of options" is a prepositional phrase that modifies *variety*.

2. That **type** of clothes is popular.
3. Those **kinds** of clothing are popular.
4. All **sorts** of trouble were awaiting us.
5. How does **waiting** for them to make a decision benefit you?

   Remark. The subject is *waiting.* The verb is *does benefit.*

4. *Here* and *there* are adverbs and thus are never subjects.

Example 116. *Here* and *there*

1. There **are** many **choices** available.

   Remark. Realizing that *choices* is the subject is easier if you mentally rearrange the sentence: "Many choices are available there."

2. There **is** only one **thing** left to do.
3. There **are** a **hat and** a **shirt** on the table.
4. Here **is** the only **book** you need.
5. Here **are** the only **books** you need.

Often, sentences such as those in example 116 are wordy. Try to rephrase them.

Example 117. Rewriting to eliminate *here* or *there*

1. Many choices are available.
2. Only one thing is left to do.
3. A hat and a shirt are on the table.

1.11.2 Guidelines for determining number

To decide whether something is singular or plural, just ask yourself whether it is considered one thing or more than one thing. The following guidelines will help you answer this question.

1. Something that corresponds to multiple nouns joined by *and* should be plural, if the nouns refer to different things.

Example 118.

Alpha, beta, and delta **are** popular Greek letters. **They** occur frequently.

2. A singular expression can sometimes end in -*s* or contain the word *and*. At the same time, there are many plural expressions that do not end in -*s*.

Example 119.

1. Divide and conquer **is** a common technique.

    Remark. "Divide and conquer" names a single technique.

2. Good news **is** being reported.

3. Our chairman and CEO **is** here.

    Remark. The chairman and CEO are the same person. If they were different people, a plural verb would be appropriate.

If awkwardness results from using *and* with a singular verb, try using a word that more precisely expresses the relationship between nouns.

Example 120.

Less specific: Working hard and succeeding was satisfying.

More specific: Succeeding after working hard was satisfying.

Less specific: Rice and lentils was served.

More specific: Rice with lentils was served.

3. *Each, every, either,* and *neither* refer to individuals within a group and are thus always considered singular, no matter how many individuals there might be. Beware that some of these words can function as adverbs and do not affect agreement when doing so.

Example 121.

1. **Is either** of the batteries working?

2. **Neither** of us **is** a student.

3. **Every** car, **every** truck, and **every** plane **is** carefully inspected.

4. **Each** of the choices **has** unique advantages.

5. The **teams** each **receive** an additional timeout.

    Remark. *Each* modifies the verb *receive* and does not affect the subject.

4. Collective nouns are singular if thought of as a unit. However, you can treat them as plural if you wish to refer to their individual elements.

Example 122.

1. The team **is** on a trip right now.

   Remark. *Team* is a collective noun regarded as singular.

2. The committee **are** discussing the matter.

   Remark. The sentence refers to the members of the committee.

3. The members of the committee **are** discussing the matter.

   Remark. You can always refer to the members explicitly if awkwardness results from treating the collective noun as plural.

4. Over 98 percent of the population **is** literate.

   Remark. The literate proportion of the population is considered a group.

5. Over 25 percent of the population **are** doctors.

   Remark. We are referring to the individuals in part of the population. The complement *doctors* suggests that the subject is considered plural.

Be consistent in how you numerically regard a collective noun within a particular sentence.

Example 123.

Awkward: The couple **completes their** trip around the world.

Remark. *Couple* is associated with a singular verb and a plural pronoun.

Better: The couple **completes its** trip around the world.

Remark. *Couple* is consistently regarded as singular.

You should try to be consistent throughout your entire composition, but you can change how you regard the number of a collective noun if you think doing so is sensible.

5. Though it may involve many people, an organization is still a single, impersonal entity.

Example 124.

Wrong: The **Red Cross** redesigned **their** logo.

Right: The **Red Cross** redesigned **its** logo.

Wrong: The **Red Cross, who** redesigned its logo...

Right: The **Red Cross, which** redesigned its logo...

6. Treat pronouns ending in *one*, *thing*, and *body* as singular.

Example 125.

Wrong: **Anyone** signing up should know what commitment **they** are making.

Right: **Anyone** signing up should know what commitment **he or she** is making.

Right: **Everyone** must think carefully about what **he or she** is doing.

Unfortunately, much awkwardness results from having to treat *everyone, anyone, no one*, etc. as singular even when they clearly refer to something plural. Other difficulties stem from trying to account for both genders with singular pronouns.

Example 126.

Right: Everybody **is** working diligently, and I thank **him** or **her** for **his** or **her** efforts.
Remark. The sentence is correct, but it is also awkward because of attempts to account for both genders.

Wrong: Everybody **is** working diligently, and I thank **them** for **their** efforts.
Remark. Using *everybody* with the singular verb *is* and the plural pronouns *them* and *their* makes no sense.

We recommend simply avoiding *everyone* and other troublesome pronouns whenever a good alternative exists. Instead of using *everybody* or *everyone* to refer to all the people in a group, say something such as "all the people."

Example 127.

All the people **are** working diligently, and I thank **them** for **their** efforts.

7. *Such, all, any, more, most, none*, and *some*, as well as other terms that convey the idea of proportion, take on the number of whatever you are describing with them.

Example 128.

1. **Most** of the water **has** evaporated.
   Remark. *Water* is singular, so *most* is singular, and *has* is the appropriate verb.

2. **Most** of the people **have** gone.
   Remark. *People* is plural, so *most* is plural, and *have* is the appropriate verb.

3. **All are** taking the examination tomorrow.
   Remark. *All* probably refers to people, so it is plural.

4. There were many people at the conference. **All** that I met **were** highly educated.
   Remark. *All* is referring to people, so it is plural.

This guideline is intuitive. When you speak of "some of the water," you are still talking about water, which is singular. Thus, "some of the water" is singular. When you speak of "some of the people," you are talking about people, and thus "some of the people" is plural. This reasoning applies to any word that conveys the idea of proportion (e.g. *percent, percentage, majority, minority, fraction*). However, note that "the percentage" is always singular. It refers to a statistic — a single number.

Example 129.

1. **The percentage** of college graduates **has** risen.
2. One **percent** of the people **are** wearing hats.
3. A small **percentage** of the people **are** wearing hats.
4. Twenty **percent** of the power **remains.**
5. A small **percentage** of the power **remains.**
6. **Half choose** to study engineering.

   Remark. We can assume *half* refers to people, so the verb is plural.

Note that in a sentence such as "one percent of the people are wearing hats," the verb does not agree with the object of the preposition (*people* in this case). *Percent* is still the subject of *are*; the prepositional phrase merely clarifies whether *percent* is singular or plural.

8. When *all* refers to an entirety, it is singular.

Example 130. *All* referring to an entirety

1. **All was** well.

   Remark. In this example, *all* means *everything.*

2. **All** they could figure out **was** the math questions.

   Remark. All refers to the entirety of what they could figure out.

3. **All** they took on their trip **was** a few shirts and a flashlight.

   Remark. All refers to the entirety of what they took on the trip.

9. Parenthetical elements do not affect the number of a subject. They can be set off by commas, dashes, or parentheses or be indicated by expressions such as:

- *as well as*
- *including*
- *(along) with*
- *in addition to*

Example 131.

1. **She**, as well as all her friends, **is** going on vacation.
2. My **professor**, in addition to my classmates, **is** going to be there.

3. **I**, along with my coworkers, **am** attending the meeting.

4. My **assistant**, as well as my supervisor, **is** attending the meeting.

Often, repositioning the parenthetical material makes the sentence less awkward.

Example 132.

Original: My professor, in addition to my classmates, is going to be there.

Rephrased: In addition to my classmates, my professor is going to be there.

10. Again, number is just a matter of whether something is being thought of as one or more than one. To determine the number of an expression, consider its meaning rather than its form.

Example 133. Using meaning instead of form

1. **Physics is** a challenging topic.
   Remark. Physics is the name of a subject.

2. The **physics** of a granular fluid **are** complex.
   Remark. Physics refers to multiple physical properties.

3. **Statistics interests** me.
   Remark. Statistics is the name of a subject.

4. The **statistics** we calculated **interest** me.
   Remark. Statistics refers to various numbers derived from a data set.

5. Two **decades is** a long time to sleep.
   Remark. Two decades refers to one period of time.

6. Those two **decades were** marked by astounding technological growth.
   Remark. We are referring to the decades as separate entities.

7. Three **people are** here.

8. Three **people is** not enough for a football team.
   Remark. The three people are considered a unit.

9. Three **milliliters** of water **is** enough.
   Remark. "Three milliliters of water" is one thing, not three things.

10. Three **dollars is** not enough to buy a football team.
    Remark. A sum of money is considered one thing.

11. Those three **dollars were** examined for signs of forgery.
    Remark. The dollars are considered separate entities.

12. A growing **number** of scientists **are** searching for an explanation.

    Remark. The number is not searching — the scientists are. "A growing number of" qualifies *scientists.*

13. The **number** of scientists investigating this topic **has** greatly increased.

14. An **average** of 300,000 cases **are** reported each year.

    Remark. "On average, 300,000 cases are reported each year" is better.

15. The **average** of 300,000 cases **has** not changed.

16. **Taxes was** the main issue.

    Remark. Taxes refers to a general concept rather than to specific instances. Using *tax* or *taxation* would convey the same idea less awkwardly.

Focusing on the meaning of an expression will help you out in numerically tricky situations. Consider example 134.

Example 134. Which verb in brackets should you choose?

One in three people here [is | are] psychic.

Remark. You would say "one in three people" only if you were talking about more than one person, so you could argue that the subject is plural and that *are* is the appropriate verb.

Remark. More accurately, though, the writer is dividing the people into groups of three and stating that one in each group is psychic. By this reasoning, the subject is singular, and *is* is the appropriate verb.

Example 135.

Only 20% of the students are going.

Remark. Most likely, someone would say "20% of the students" only if it referred to more than one person, so using a plural verb makes sense.

Remark. If there are exactly five students, perhaps you could say "only 20% of the students is going," but you really should just say "only one of the five students is going."

Example 136.

More than one student are going.

Remark. "More than one" is clearly plural, but "one student are going" sounds bizarre. You can express the idea more simply and less awkwardly by saying "several students are going" or "multiple students are going."

A friendly reminder: If following a rule makes your writing awkward, consider rephrasing. If the grammar of a particular sentence is so complicated that you have trouble determining proper usage, look for a simpler way of expressing yourself. Extremely complicated grammar often occurs in writing that needs to be reworded.

Chapter 2

Punctuation

2.1 Periods

1. Use a period after a declarative sentence and after an imperative sentence. The previous sentence is imperative and ends with a period. The sentence you're reading now is declarative and also ends with a period.
2. Periods usually follow abbreviations (e.g. *Dr., Jan., Jr.*).
3. Periods are usually **not** found in acronyms (e.g. *FBI, UN, CERN, GRE, ACT, SEC*).

2.2 Question marks

1. Question marks go only after expressions intended to be questions (though the expressions may technically be declarations).

Example 137.

1. You really thought I would give up?

   Remark. The sentence, expressing disbelief, ends in a question mark despite technically being a declaration.

2. They said they would be ready by Monday?

   Remark. The sentence means "did they say they would be ready by Monday?" It ends in a question mark despite having the form of a declaration.

2. **Indirect questions** are considered declarations.

Example 138.

1. They asked me to help.
2. "Could you help us?" my friend asked.

   Remark. The quotation is a question, but the entire sentence is a declaration about what someone asked.

3. The symbol *(?)* indicates uncertainty. We recommend using it for factual uncertainty only.

Example 139.

1. In 1835(?), the widget was invented.
   Remark. The symbol expresses uncertainty about the correctness of the year.

2. The Invincible (?) Armada actually suffered a humiliating defeat.
   Remark. Here, the symbol conveys irony. We recommend refraining from such usage.

2.3   Exclamation marks

1. Exclamation marks go after emotional expressions (e.g. *look out!*) or strong interjections (e.g. *no!*).
2. Be sure the situation really calls for one, and don't use groups of them (e.g. *wow!!!*).
3. Refrain from combining exclamation marks with question marks (e.g. *are you serious!?*).
4. Exclamation marks are rarely used in formal writing.

2.4   Commas

Example 140 presents a paragraph with all of its commas removed. Observe how reading it, though not excessively difficult, takes noticeably more effort than reading the original paragraph, which appears in example 141.

Example 140. A paragraph with no commas

Fear that relentless pursuer hindered Dantes's efforts. He listened for any sound that might be audible and every time that he rose to the top of the water he scanned the horizon and strove to peer through the darkness. He imagined that every wave behind him was a pursuing boat and he redoubled his efforts rapidly increasing his distance from the prison but exhausting his strength. He swam on still and already the terrible dungeon had disappeared in the darkness. He could not see it but he felt its presence. An hour passed during which Dantes excited by the feeling of freedom continued to struggle through the waves.

Example 141. Example 140 with commas

Fear, that relentless pursuer, hindered Dantes's efforts. He listened for any sound that might be audible, and every time that he rose to the top of the water, he scanned the horizon and strove to peer through the darkness. He imagined that every wave behind him was a pursuing boat, and he redoubled his efforts, rapidly increasing his distance from the prison but exhausting his strength. He swam on still, and already the terrible dungeon had disappeared in the darkness. He could not see it, but he felt its presence. An hour passed, during which Dantes, excited by the feeling of freedom, continued to struggle through the waves.

Commas separate expressions and indicate pauses to aid interpretation.

Rule for comma use: Use a comma if it makes something easier to read or is essential to its meaning. Any commas that do not improve clarity should almost certainly be left out.

Reading your writing out loud and listening for natural pauses is another helpful method for determining where to place commas.

Below, we describe various ways you can use commas to improve the clarity of your writing. Keep in mind that if, in a particular situation, following our suggestions for comma use doesn't benefit your writing, you should leave the comma(s) out.

Each example titled "comparisons" presents expressions in pairs. The expressions within each pair are the same, except that commas are absent from the first one and not from the second. Notice how in each case, the presence of commas affects the meaning of the statement or makes it easier to read. Also notice that most of the situations we describe involve a series or an interruption of some kind.

1. Separate modifiers of the same expression if *and* makes sense between them.

Example 142.

Wrong: a quick agile experienced football player

Right: a quick, agile, experienced football player

Wrong: a quick, agile, experienced, football player

One would not say "an experienced and football player," so there is no comma between *experienced* and *football*. However, one could say "a quick and agile and experienced football player," so there are commas after *quick* and *agile*.

Example 143. Comparisons

It was a powerful sound argument.

It was a powerful, sound argument.

It was a brilliant secret perfectly executed strategy.

It was a brilliant, secret, perfectly executed strategy.

These three brand-new state-of-the-art gadgets are for sale.

These three brand-new, state-of-the-art gadgets are for sale.

light blue luggage

light, blue luggage

Remark. In this case, placing a comma between *light* and *blue* clarifies which word *light* modifies. To have *light* unquestionably modify *blue*, place a hyphen between the two words. With no punctuation, the phrase is vague.

2. Separate items in a list containing more than two elements. Do not omit the comma associated with the final item.

Example 144. A confusing sentence

The company has exactly two divisions: research, technology and analysis, and consulting services.

Several things are wrong with example 144. There appear to be three divisions:

- research
- technology and analysis
- consulting services

This can't be right, of course, since the sentence states that there are only two divisions. The two divisions are actually:

- research, technology, and analysis
- consulting services

Unfortunately, the writer omitted the comma after *technology* and, even worse, inserted an unnecessary comma after *analysis.* Correctly punctuated, the sentence should read:

"The company has exactly two divisions: research, technology, and analysis and consulting services."

Example 145. Comparisons

water bottles cereal boxes peanut butter and jelly sandwiches and ice cream

water, bottles, cereal, boxes, peanut butter and jelly sandwiches, and ice cream

Ensure that the statement is still clear that what has been omitted is obvious and that filling in the missing words actually results in a sensible expression.

Ensure that the statement is still clear, that what has been omitted is obvious, and that filling in the missing words actually results in a sensible expression.

I recently visited my cousins, Bill Gates and Rafael Nadal.

I recently visited my cousins, Bill Gates, and Rafael Nadal.

No punctuation is necessary for conjunctions serving as delimiters, though punctuation can help achieve a particular rhythm.

Example 146. Constructing a list

1. love, joy, peace, patience, kindness, goodness, faithfulness, gentleness, and self-control
   Remark. We constructed a list with commas and one conjunction.

2. love and joy and peace and patience and kindness and goodness and faithfulness and gentleness and self-control

Remark. We are using *and* as a delimiter.

3. love and joy and peace, and patience and kindness and goodness, and faithfulness, gentleness and self-control

Remark. We used a combination of delimiters.

Remark. The second and third methods are used only for rhetorical purposes. In general, stick with the first method.

3. Separate introductions from the rest of the sentence. Introductory verbal phrases often cause problems if not separated.

Example 147. Comparisons

Though weather conditions were highly unfavorable travel was still possible.

Though weather conditions were highly unfavorable, travel was still possible.

While I was walking around the sun set.

While I was walking around, the sun set.

Though I had plenty of time to study the exam was still difficult.

Though I had plenty of time to study, the exam was still difficult.

4. Separate appositives.

Example 148. Comparisons

The supervisors my friend and I oversee 30 people.

The supervisors, my friend and I, oversee 30 people.

5. Signal unusual word order.

Example 149. Comparisons

The answer given rather hastily turned out to be incorrect.

The answer, given rather hastily, turned out to be incorrect.

The training rigorous and difficult will help you in the end.

The training, rigorous and difficult, will help you in the end.

Not all instances of unusual word order require commas, however. Again, the use of a comma should depend on whether it aids the reader.

Example 150. Unusual word order that does not require comma use

1. Within the temple lurks an ancient and fearsome power.
2. An ancient and fearsome power within the temple lurks.

---

6. Separate a direct address. That is, set off the name of an entity that you are speaking to.

Example 151. Comparisons

Please reconsider Dr. Green as your choice may have unexpected consequences.

Please reconsider, Dr. Green, as your choice may have unexpected consequences.

Remark. We are speaking to Dr. Green.

---

7. Separate sentence modifiers.

Example 152. Comparisons

However we tried our best and succeeded.

However, we tried our best and succeeded.

The work having been completed we took a break.

The work having been completed, we took a break.

---

8. Separate nonrestrictive clauses.

Example 153. Comparisons

The guards who are familiar with the terrain will go with you.

The guards, who are familiar with the terrain, will go with you.

---

9. Separate two clauses joined by a conjunction.

Example 154. Comparisons

I helped my brother and my sister helped my parents.

I helped my brother, and my sister helped my parents.

Using a comma without a conjunction results in an error called a **comma fault**.

Example 155.

Wrong: I helped my brother, my sister helped my parents.

Right: I helped my brother, and my sister helped my parents.

Wrong: This problem is more urgent, therefore we should address it first.

Right: This problem is more urgent, and therefore we should address it first.

Comma faults are undesirable because commas typically signal appositives, inverted word order, sentence modifiers, or other constructions ultimately grouped with a particular subject-verb pairing. Using only a comma to present readers with a new, independent subject-verb pairing is generally disruptive.

Example 156. A disruptive comma fault

We redesigned the system, which was too slow, we know how important efficiency is.

Remark. The comma after *slow* suggests a continuation of the sentence, but instead, a new sentence begins. You can correct this error by changing the misused comma to a period and capitalizing *we*.

Not all comma faults are disruptive, however.

Example 157. An acceptable comma fault

You're going to be there, aren't you?

Remark. Such a sentence is poorly constructed unless you intend to use it for dialogue. The second clause is redundant; you could ask the same question by saying "are you going to be there?"

10. Separate moderate interjections. Powerful interjections require exclamation marks instead of commas (see section 2.3).

Example 158. Comparisons

No I'm fine.

No, I'm fine.

Oh I see.

Oh, I see.

11. Separate speaker attributions from quotations in conversation. See the section on quotation marks for more information.
12. Commas can set off certain statements the writer considers parenthetical, though we recommend using parentheses or dashes for such statements.

Example 159. Comparisons

My friend the person that I mentioned earlier went with me.

My friend, the person that I mentioned earlier, went with me.

Notice from example 159 that a clause can be considered parenthetical even if it is restrictive.

13. Indicate pauses that represent missing words. Be careful, though — omitting words and assuming the reader will fill them in can make your writing difficult to understand.

Example 160. Comparisons

I used the umbrella to shield myself from sunlight not from rain.

I used the umbrella to shield myself from sunlight, not from rain.
Remark. The comma indicates a pause that represents the word *and.*

The people there are delightful; the atmosphere peaceful; the landscape beautiful.

The people there are delightful; the atmosphere, peaceful; the landscape, beautiful.
Remark. The commas indicate pauses that stand for the word *is.*

14. Separate adjacent names within an address.

Example 161. Comparisons

12345 Westport Street Metropolis Washington 98765

12345 Westport Street, Metropolis, Washington 98765

15. Separate adjacent numbers within dates.

Example 162. Comparisons

January 15 2073

January 15, 2073

---

16. In letters, use a comma after the closing (e.g. *Sincerely,*) and after an informal salutation (e.g. *Dear friends,*).

Commas are frequently used where they are not needed. If you follow the guidelines detailed above, you should be able to avoid unnecessarily using commas. Notice that the underlined commas in example 163 do not aid interpretation and that the sentences are better off without them.

Example 163. Unnecessary commas

1. The training (though it was difficult), helped us a lot in the end.
   Remark. Don't place a comma after something enclosed by parentheses unless placing a comma there would have made sense without the parenthetical expression.

2. The obstacles standing in our way for so many years, were finally overcome.
   Remark. Separating the subject from the verb is pointless.

3. We competed for, but did not win the gold medal.
   Remark. Separating the preposition *for* from its complement is pointless.

4. We competed for but did not win, the gold medal.
   Remark. Separating the verb *win* from its complement is pointless.

5. We trained intensely for many years, and were able to set new world records.
   Remark. "Were able to set new world records" cannot be a sentence, so no comma is necessary.

6. A fast, experienced, famous, athlete won first place.
   Remark. The final modifier in a series does not need to be separated from what it modifies.

7. The renovations were designed to improve, not the appearance of the building, but its safety.
   Remark. The conjunction *not...but* isn't joining clauses, so no commas are necessary.

8. The renovations were designed to improve, not only the appearance of the building, but also its safety.
   Remark. The conjunction *not only...but also* isn't joining clauses, so no commas are necessary.

9. I fell asleep, but, in my defense, your lecture was really boring.
   Remark. Separating the conjunction from a short introduction is pointless.

Of course, you can use commas to perform the functions in example 163 if the rule for comma use (page 71) is met. See the next example.

Example 164.

1. We scheduled the parade for today, but, the weather having suddenly turned bad, we had to cancel it.
   Remark. A comma may be helpful between a conjunction and a long introductory phrase.

2. Those that do, do so at their own risk.
   Remark. The separation of the subject and the verb makes the sentence easier to read.

Commas are not required to separate all instances of repeated words, however.

Example 165. The sentence below does not require a comma.

They are people people respect.

Remark. "They are people that people respect" or "they are respected people" would be better.

2.5 Hyphens

1. Join parts of a word that appear on different lines of text. Be sure the word is divided between syllables, which can be thought of as natural units of pronunciation.

Example 166.

Right: Wrong:

Be sure the word is di-   Be sure the word i-
vided between syllables.   s divided between syllables.

2. Express the spelling of an expression, one letter at a time (e.g. *s-e-v-e-n*).
3. Separate the numbers in a range or the scores of a game (e.g. *the years 1512-1520; the final score is 14-10*). Some suggest avoiding such usage in formal writing. Also, the hyphen stands for the word *to* and does not make sense with *between*.

Example 167.

1. Wrong: between 10-50
   Remark. "Between 10 to 50" is nonstandard.

2. Right: between 10 and 50

4. Clarify the meaning of an expression.

Example 168.

1. re-sign: to sign again
2. resign: to leave a position voluntarily
3. re-cover: to cover again
4. recover: to regain possession of
5. re-call: to call again
6. recall: to remember; to order to return

Example 169.

1. a photo of a man eating fish
   Remark. a photo of a person

2. a photo of a man-eating fish
   Remark. a photo of a fish

3. a big business regulation
   Remark. a big regulation for business

4. a big-business regulation
   Remark. a regulation for large businesses

5. Make a suffix or prefix less awkward (e.g. *re-examine*, *de-emphasize*).
6. Have multiple words act as a single term (e.g. *built-in*, *rip-off*, *in-laws*, *light-blue*).

Example 170. Identifying words that act as a single term

1. The information was provided in a paper cut-out.
   Remark. Together, *cut* and *out* act as the name of something.

2. Cut out the excess.
   Remark. *Cut* is a verb; *out* is a modifier. No hyphen is necessary.

3. a light-blue backpack
   Remark. The hyphen ensures that the reader does not associate *light* with *backpack*.

4. The container is three-quarters full.
   Remark. *Three* and *quarters* modify *full* together.

5. We used three quarters of the material.
   Remark. A quarter is a thing — 25% of something. We have used three of them.

6. The container is ninety-nine one hundredths full.
   Remark. A hyphen between *ninety-nine* and *one hundredths* would be confusing, so one does not appear.

7. an open-minded person
   Remark. *Open* and *minded* form a unit.

8. an extremely thoughtful person
   Remark. Usually, no hyphen is necessary between an adverb and the adjective it modifies.

9. an ear-splitting noise
   Remark. *Ear* and *splitting* describe *noise* as a unit.

10. a ninety-year-old building
    Remark. *Ninety*, *year*, and *old* modify *building* as a whole.

When do you use "well known" instead of "well-known"? How come "well-known" is not always hyphenated, but "all-knowing" always is? Why do you hyphenate "half-baked" but not "half brother"? There are dozens of hyphenation conventions (and exceptions to go with them). Even worse, traditions differ from one version of English to another (e.g. British English and American English have different hyphenation standards). To deal with this tedious situation, we recommend the following:

1. Ignore the maze of conventions. A hyphen should improve the clarity or readability of your writing. Use a hyphen if you think doing so is beneficial; otherwise, don't bother using one.

2. If you must strictly follow conventions in a particular situation, consult a dictionary or style manual to decide whether you should hyphenate a term. Conventions tend to change with time and location, so using a reference accepted by your audience is best.

2.6   Dashes

1. Signal (1) an abrupt change in thought or (2) an afterthought.

2. Suggest "namely" or "in other words."

3. Set off parenthetical information (just as parentheses do).

4. Signify stammering or interrupted speech.

5. Interrupt quotations to provide additional information.

Example 171.

1. I was unconscious at the time — as far as I could tell, anyway.

2. I saw quite a few people there — family, friends, coworkers, etc.

3. Set off parenthetical information — just as parentheses do.

4. Set off — as parentheses do — parenthetical information.

5. "But I — you — how did you — ?"

6. "We found what we were looking for" — they looked quite excited now — "in the last place we expected."

6. Dashes should not enclose more than one sentence.

7. Dashes are traditionally represented by two hyphens.

8. Dashes, unlike parentheses, do not have to occur in pairs.

9. Use dashes sparingly. Frequent interruptions can make your writing disorganized.

2.7   Parentheses and brackets

1. Parentheses enclose interruptions. Generally, such interruptions serve to qualify, explain, elaborate, or rename. Parentheses, like dashes, should be used sparingly.

2. Parentheses (as opposed to commas and dashes) can properly enclose multiple sentences, though we advise against using parentheses in this way.

Example 172. Using parentheses to enclose more than one sentence

After we finished unpacking (it took nearly 3 hours. We obviously brought too many things), we decided to go hiking.

3. Create numbered lists.

Example 173.

Error 104 indicates that (1) your drivers are outdated, (2) you are missing a configuration file, or (3) compatibility mode is unnecessary.

4. Use brackets (not parentheses) to denote annotations or changes you make to quotations.

Example 174.

1. The author writes, "The term [chiaroscuro] is Italian for *bright-dark*."
   Remark. Our annotation is bracketed.

2. The author writes, "[Chiaroscuro] is Italian for *bright-dark*."
   Remark. We changed "the term" to "Chiaroscuro" and denoted our change with brackets.

3. The author states that "[t]he term is Italian for *bright-dark*."
   Remark. The author originally capitalized *the*, but we made the word lowercase to fit it in with our sentence. Our change is bracketed.

We recommend preserving quotations as much as possible. Make annotations rather than changes.

5. Nested parenthetical material (i.e. parenthetical material within parenthetical material) should be delimited by symbols different from those enclosing the immediately surrounding parenthetical material.

Example 175.

This sentence (at first — fortunately, only at first — it is somewhat confusing) has parenthetical material.
Remark. The parenthetical statement "at first it is somewhat confusing" contains the parenthetical expression "fortunately, only at first." Dashes set off the nested statement, whereas parentheses set off the containing statement. If you wanted, you could instead use dashes for the containing statement and parentheses for the nested one.

Parenthetical material included in a nested statement set off by dashes could be enclosed by another pair of parentheses, and so on. The structure would look like this:

(words — words (words) words — words)

2.8   Apostrophes

1. Create the possessive forms of most nouns.
2. Form contractions (e.g. *do not = don't, could not = couldn't, I have = I've*). The apostrophe stands in for the missing letters. Some suggest avoiding contractions in formal writing.
3. Form the plurals of letters, numerals, symbols, and references to expressions themselves.

Example 176.

1. *Gadsby* — a 50,000 word book — does not contain any *e*'s.
2. Your research paper has too many *&*'s and not nearly enough *the*'s.

2.9   Colons

1. Follow a formal salutation.

Example 177. A formal salutation

To whom it may concern:

2. Separate hours and minutes in descriptions of time (e.g. *5:30*).
3. Introduce lists, quotations, and clauses. Introducing one clause with another is appropriate if the second elaborates on, clarifies, reiterates, or explains the first one. A clause joined by a colon to another clause does not have to begin with a capital letter.
4. Separate a title from a subtitle (e.g. *Time Travel: A Practical Guide*).
5. Don't use a colon if your statement correctly conveys your intended meaning without one.

Example 178.

1. You will need the following items: a first aid kit, a flare gun, and a parachute.
   Remark. This use of the colon is correct. The sentence makes no sense without the colon.
2. They said: "Run fast; run far."
   Remark. The first word of the clause following the colon is capitalized because of quotation conventions, not because of the colon.
3. There was only one option left: they had to land the airplane themselves.
   Remark. The colon is appropriate because the first clause introduces the second one. Notice that the second clause does not have to begin with a capital letter.
4. Be sure to bring: a first aid kit, a flare gun, and a parachute.
   Remark. This use of the colon is incorrect. The sentence makes perfect sense without the colon.

2.10 Semicolons

1. Join closely related independent clauses.

2. Semicolons should be used between clauses joined by adverbs that resemble conjunctions (e.g. *thus, then, however, consequently, therefore, also, moreover, besides, indeed, nevertheless*).

3. Separate elements that themselves have commas, if using commas would cause confusion or make the statement difficult to read.

Example 179.

1. Money is not a root of evil; the love of money is.

   Remark. The semicolon separates two closely related independent clauses.

2. The odds are heavily against us; nevertheless, we must try.

   Remark. The semicolon separates two closely related independent clauses, the second of which begins with the adverb *nevertheless.*

3. We met Smith, the president; the vice president; and the treasurer.

   Remark. Changing all the semicolons to commas would imply that we met four people, not three.

4. We analyzed all the information, but because it was so disorganized, the process took much longer than it normally does.

   Remark. Either a comma or a semicolon could be used after *information,* though usage of the semicolon before a coordinating conjunction is now uncommon. Even if we use a comma, the sentence is easy to decipher, so using one is acceptable.

5. We analyzed all the information, which, despite being organized, was difficult to work with; we summarized our findings and, in accordance with organizational guidelines, detailed them in the last section of the report; and we submitted the report for publication.

   Remark. In order to separate many statements that themselves contain commas, we must use semicolons. Otherwise, the sentence becomes difficult to decipher.

2.11 Quotation marks

1. Enclose someone else's words. A **direct quotation** represents someone else's exact words. An **indirect quotation** conveys the meaning, but not the exact wording, of someone else's statement.

Example 180.

1. They said, "We faced difficult circumstances."

   Remark. a direct quotation

2. They said that their circumstances were difficult.

   Remark. an indirect quotation

2. Enclose expressions used in some special way.

- Place quotation marks around the titles of "short works" such as articles, songs, book chapters, short stories, and poems. The title of any other work (e.g. books, plays, movies, paintings) should be underlined or italicized.
- Quotation marks can enclose nicknames (e.g. *Kyle "The Yellow Dart" Smith*).
- Quotation marks or italics can signal expressions being discussed or unfamiliar terms.
  - Generally, only the first instance of an unfamiliar term is italicized or has quotation marks.
  - For expressions being discussed, italicizing is usually a better option than using quotation marks. Quotation marks can become awkward at times, such as when several expressions under discussion appear in a row.

Example 181.

1. "Pentasyllabic" is a term that refers to itself.
2. *Pentasyllabic* is a term that refers to itself.
3. A term that refers to itself is "self-referential."
4. A term that refers to itself is *self-referential.*
5. *English, sesquipedalian, adjectival,* and *extant* are other self-referential terms.
6. "English," "sesquipedalian," "adjectival," and "extant" are other self-referential terms.

- Quotation marks can enclose figurative expressions (e.g. *"borrowed" words*).
- Call attention to a special expression in one way only. If a special expression is already set off by quotation marks, do not italicize it or introduce it with an expression such as "so-called."

Example 182.

Redundant: The graph contains a so-called "saddle point."

Redundant: The graph contains a so-called *saddle point.*

Redundant: The graph contains a "*saddle po*int."

Better: The graph contains a so-called saddle point.

Better: The graph contains a "saddle point."

Better: The graph contains a *saddle point.*

We recommend using quotation marks only for the purposes detailed above. Refrain from using them to convey irony or disdain.

2.11.1   Conventions for quotations

1. When writing a line of dialogue, begin the quotation with a capital letter, and use commas or some other appropriate punctuation to separate both the quoted text and the attribution from the rest of the sentence.

Example 183. Dialogue

1. "Please hand your assignment in by Friday," the professor wrote.
2. "Three examinations will determine the final grade," said the professor.
3. The professor then thought, "How did I get here?"
4. "How did I get here?" asked the professor.
5. "Don't move!" they shouted.
6. "What about the —" they began.
7. "What about the..." they began.
8. They replied: "We're not sure."
9. "This is wonderful news," I said, and smiled cheerfully.
10. "This is wonderful news!" I said, and smiled cheerfully.
11. I said, "This is wonderful news," and smiled cheerfully.
12. I said, "This is wonderful news!" and smiled cheerfully.
13. "This is wonderful news," I said, and then, "We should celebrate."
14. I said, "Wonderful!" and smiled cheerfully.

If a quotation blends in with the rest of its sentence and doesn't seem like part of a dialogue, separating the quotation and its attribution from the surrounding text is unnecessary. If you aren't working with dialogue, a quoted fragment does not require capitalization, but people disagree on whether a quoted sentence does. Go with what your particular audience expects, and be consistent.

Whether something qualifies as dialogue is sometimes unclear. If you think your line of possible dialogue is better without extra commas, feel free to leave them out.

Example 184. Not dialogue

1. The professor said that "three examinations will determine the final grade."
2. They said that "a large proportion" came from anonymous benefactors.
3. Not until I said "All of you are going to fail" did the students pay attention.
4. Their reply was "We don't know."
5. "Maybe" was their reply.
6. They never said "We agree." They said "We'll think about it."
7. They said something like "it doesn't matter."
8. I thought they said "we don't know."

2. If a quotation in a line of dialogue is divided, each segment should be set off by some kind of punctuation aside from the quotation marks. If the quotation is divided into separate sentences, you must use terminal punctuation and capitalization accordingly. Use dashes to set off an interruption that is not an attribution.

Example 185.

1. "The results of your examination," said the professor, "surprised me."
2. "The results of your examination surprised me," said the professor. "No one has ever received a negative score. You also misspelled your own name."

3. In a dialogue, begin a new paragraph whenever the speaker changes. Place information relevant to the quotation in the same paragraph as the quotation.

Example 186.

"So you did, old fellow!" said the others.

"We must break the door down!" he said.

She called out as loudly as she could, "You'll be sorry!" There was a dead silence instantly, and she thought to herself, "I wonder what they will do next! If they had any sense, they'd take the roof off."

After a minute or two, they began moving about again, and she heard the man say, "A barrowful will do, to begin with."

"A barrowful of what?" she thought; but she had not long to doubt, for the next moment a shower of little pebbles came rattling in at the window, and some of them hit her in the face. "I'll put a stop to this," she said to herself, and shouted out, "You'd better not do that again!" which produced another dead silence.

She noticed with some surprise that the pebbles were all turning into little cakes as they lay on the floor, and a bright idea came into her head. "If I eat one of these cakes," she thought, "it's sure to make some change in my size; and as it can't possibly make me larger, it must make me smaller, I suppose."

4. Dialogue consisting of nothing but very short statements can be contained in one paragraph.

Example 187.

"You couldn't..." "I could." "You didn't." "I did." "You wouldn't!" "I would."

5. For a quotation that spans more than one paragraph:
   (a) Place an opening quotation mark where the quotation begins.
   (b) Place an opening quotation mark at the beginning of each subsequent paragraph containing part of the quotation.
   (c) Place a closing quotation mark where the quotation ends.

Example 188. A quotation that spans multiple paragraphs

This example illustrates proper punctuation. "Suppose the quotation begins with this sentence. It begins with opening quotation marks as usual.

"Each paragraph after the one that begins the quotation starts with opening quotation marks.

"A closing quotation mark appears only after the quotation ends. Suppose it ends here." Notice that the second paragraph does not have any closing quotation marks.

6. Extensive quotations from writings are indicated by indentation on both sides rather than by quotation marks. If there are several paragraphs, each one can begin with an additional indentation.

Example 189.

The story continues:

> The vague disquietude which prevailed amongst the spectators had so much affected one of the crowd that he did not await the arrival of the vessel in harbour, but jumping into a small skiff, desired to be pulled alongside the Pharaon, which he reached as she rounded the creek of La Réserve.
>
> When the young man on board saw this individual approach, he left his station by the pilot, and came, hat in hand, to the side of the ship's bulwarks.
>
> He was a fine, tall, slim young fellow, with black eyes, and hair as dark as the raven's wing; and his whole appearance bespoke that calmness and resolution peculiar to men accustomed from their cradle to contend with danger.

A conversation involving several central characters begins after this description. Read the rest of the book if you're interested.

7. Some advise making the capitalization of your quotations identical to that of the original text, while some suggest changing capitalization to fit your needs. Follow whatever convention you think is better, but be consistent. We recommend altering capitalization as needed and indicating the changes with brackets.

8. A direct quotation should agree grammatically with the rest of its sentence. If it does not, then modify your sentence, change which text is quoted, or do not use a direct quotation at all.

Example 190.

1. Wrong: According to the article, they had "wrote numerous essays on the subject."
2. Right: According to the article, they had written "numerous essays on the subject."
3. Right: According to the article, they "wrote numerous essays on the subject."
4. Right: According to the article, they had written numerous essays on the subject.

9. Alternate delimiters with nested quotations. Start out with whichever your audience expects.

Example 191. Nested quotations

The professor said, "I received your message about 'not being able to read "Judgment under Uncertainty." ' "

The professor said, 'I received your message about "not being able to read 'Judgment under Uncertainty.' " '

2.12   Ellipses

1. *Ellipsis* (plural, *ellipses*) refers either to the omission of words or to a punctuation mark (...) indicating such an omission. In this book, *ellipsis* and *ellipses* refer to punctuation marks only.

2. Omissions in the middle of a quotation should always be indicated; omissions at the endpoints do not have to be indicated if you think doing so is unimportant or if you believe the omissions are obvious.

Example 192 illustrates the use of ellipses by quoting from the following paragraphs:

> Take a rectangular strip of paper. Give one end a 180 degree twist and join it to the other end to form a loop. The strange object that results, called a Möbius strip, has only one "side." To see this for yourself, draw a line down the middle of the strip, parallel to the edge. It's actually possible to travel between any two points on a Möbius strip without crossing an edge.
>
> Cut the strip down the line you drew. What happens then? Somehow, you get an ordinary loop twice as long as the one you started with. However, cutting a Möbius strip lengthwise about a third of the way from the edge will result in two structures. One of them is a Möbius strip, and the other is an ordinary loop.
>
> The Möbius strip is named after August Ferdinand Möbius, but it was first discovered by mathematician Johann Benedict Listing. Actually, Möbius independently discovered the structure several weeks after Listing.

Example 192. Using ellipses

1. "Take a...strip of paper."
   Remark. We omitted a word in the middle of a sentence.

2. The authors then ask you to join the ends after a "180 degree twist."
   Remark. The presence of an omission is obvious, so no indication is necessary.

3. The authors then ask you to join the ends after a "...180 degree twist... ."
   Remark. an example of correctly used but unnecessary ellipses

4. The goal is to "...form a loop."
   Remark. a quotation with the beginning omitted

5. "The strange object that results, called a Möbius strip, has only one 'side.' ...It's actually possible to travel between any two points on a Möbius strip without crossing an edge."
   Remark. We omitted a sentence between two other sentences.

6. The authors ask you to "[g]ive one end a 180 degree twist... ."
   Remark. We omitted text at the end of the quotation.

7. The authors ask you to draw a line along "[t]he strange object that results... ."

> *Remark.* The statement ends in a period even if the quotation is not a sentence. In the original text, *the* begins with a capital letter, but we made the word lowercase so that it would fit with our sentence (the change is bracketed).

8. "The Möbius strip is named after August Ferdinand Möbius, but...Möbius independently discovered the structure several weeks after Listing."

   Remark. We omitted the end of one sentence and the beginning of another.

9. "The Möbius strip is named after August Ferdinand Möbius. ...Möbius independently discovered the structure several weeks after Listing."

   Remark. We omitted the end of one sentence and the beginning of another. Despite the omission, "the Möbius strip is named after August Ferdinand Möbius" is still a sentence, so it ends with a period.

10. "The strange object that results, called a Möbius strip, has only one 'side.' ...it was first discovered by mathematician Johann Benedict Listing."

    Remark. We have two complete sentences despite the omission. We could have capitalized *it* to make the statement easier to read or to make the capitalization conform to our sentence. If we wanted to indicate the change, we would write it as *[I]t.*

Remark. The following examples demonstrate how you can preserve the punctuation of the original text if you need to.

11. "Cut the strip down the line... . What happens...?...[Y]ou get an ordinary loop. ..."

12. "To see this..., draw a line down the middle of the strip, parallel to the edge."

13. "However,...[o]ne of them is a Möbius strip, and the other is an ordinary loop."

3. Ellipses can replace omitted text of any length. The omission could be as short as one word or as long as several paragraphs.

4. If you are presenting a quotation in its original paragraph structure:

   (a) Ellipsis points (preceded by a period, if you think it helps) should appear when the end of a paragraph has been omitted and the quotation then continues with a new paragraph. This notation is adequate even if many paragraphs have been excluded. The same notation is also used when the end of the paragraph has not been omitted but one or more complete paragraphs have been skipped before the quotation continues.

   (b) Ellipsis points should appear if a paragraph begins with an omission. If the end of one paragraph and the beginning of the resuming one have been omitted, ellipsis points should appear in both places.

Example 193. Presenting a quotation in its original paragraph structure

> Take a rectangular strip of paper. Give one end a 180 degree twist and join it to the other end to form a loop. The strange object that results, called a Möbius strip, has only one "side." To see this for yourself, draw a line down the middle of the strip, parallel to the edge. ...
> ...it was first discovered by mathematician Johann Benedict Listing. Actually, Möbius independently discovered the structure several weeks after Listing.

5. Omitting words to change the meaning of the original text is frowned upon.

6. You may include punctuation from the original text with your quotation if doing so improves readability or if you must accurately represent the quotation's original punctuation.

7. Ellipses can indicate speech that trails off or pauses (e.g. "I wonder if...maybe...").

Example 194.

"Let me see if I have this right. ...Even though you've never done any exercise in your life...you're going to run a marathon? Sure..."

"You don't seem to think it's a good idea. ..."

Notice from example 194 that:

- Pauses between sentences do not affect terminal punctuation.
- An incomplete sentence that trails off does not have a period.
- A complete sentence that trails off does have terminal punctuation.

Use ellipses to indicate manner of speech only if you are sure they cannot be interpreted as representing omissions.

Example 195.

"Actually...no one knows."

Remark. The reader cannot be sure whether the ellipsis represents a pause or an omission.

---

8. Make sure that ellipsis points indicate either omission or manner of speech. Do not use them without purpose, and do not use them to perform the functions of other punctuation marks.

Example 196. Improper use of ellipses

1. Nevertheless...we will continue.
   Remark. A comma should be used instead of an ellipsis.

2. Any arrangement is fine...just be reasonable.
   Remark. A period, semicolon, or dash should be used instead of an ellipsis.

3. We could use the first one...or the second one.
   Remark. The ellipsis serves no purpose and should be eliminated.

2.13   Slash

1. Avoid using the slash to join terms. Instead, clearly express the relationships between them.

Using a slash to join terms is often a sign of muddled thinking. Is a "quirk/phobia/fatal flaw" one of them or all of them? Are the three terms merely possibilities, only one of which is correct, or are they equally viable alternatives? It is likely the writer himself does not know.

Example 197.

Unclear: Make your speech inspiring/challenging.

Clear: Make your speech inspiring and challenging.

Clear: Make your speech inspiring or challenging.

Clear: Make your speech inspiring or challenging or both.

Unclear: tomato/onion soup

Clear: tomato soup or onion soup

2. The slash can be used to express ratios, rates, and other things related to mathematical division (e.g. *kilometers/second, 1/2*).

3. The slash can also be used to signal line breaks when quoting poetry.

2.14 Combining punctuation

Some points to keep in mind:

1. Periods, question marks, and exclamation marks are able to signal the end of a sentence and are known as terminal punctuation.

2. The ellipsis is not considered terminal punctuation.

3. Sometimes, what looks like punctuation is actually part of a term. Such marks should not be considered part of your statement's punctuation. For instance, periods in abbreviations should not be considered terminal punctuation.

Example 198.

Unconventional: Did you mean Jr. or Sr?

Conventional: Did you mean Jr. or Sr.?

4. From quoted text, any punctuation that needs to be represented accurately should not be considered part of your statement's punctuation.

Example 199.

The opening sentence, "What do you mean???," illustrates the author's excessive use of question marks.

Generally, place punctuation where it logically belongs:

1. Place punctuation within quotation marks if it is part of the quotation; place punctuation outside quotation marks if it is part of the statement to which the quotation belongs. The same logic applies to placing punctuation relative to parentheses. Generally, place colons, semicolons, commas, and terminal punctuation outside quotation marks and parentheses. However, keep in mind:

   (a) **Closing** quotation marks can logically follow commas and terminal punctuation.
   (b) **Closing** parentheses can logically follow terminal punctuation.

Example 200.

Nothing is "foolproof"; someone always builds a better fool.

Nothing is "foolproof" (or "idiot proof"); someone always builds a better fool (or idiot).

Nothing is "foolproof" (how could you think otherwise?).

Is anything "foolproof" (whatever that means)?

Unfortunately, "nothing is foolproof (no matter how simple)."

---

2. Commas and periods can be placed where they logically belong in relation to closing quotation marks, but some prefer always placing closing quotation marks last.

Example 201.

Logical: According to an old saying, if you make something "foolproof", then "someone will build a better fool."

Logical: According to an old saying, if you make something "foolproof", then someone will build "a better fool".

Conventional: According to an old saying, if you make something "foolproof," then someone will build "a better fool."

---

3. Always place parentheses, quotation marks, brackets, and ellipses where they are logically required.

There are some situations in which punctuation is not placed logically. Exceptions to logical placement are often made for the sake of improved typographical appearance. You should be able to combine punctuation correctly in almost all situations if you remember the major exceptions detailed below and assume logical placement otherwise.

1. Use only one punctuation mark to terminate or set off text within quotation marks. Marks that can always be placed where needed don't count as separators or terminators.

Example 202.

Conventional: Did the bystander say "how are you"?

Conventional: Did the bystander say "how are you?"

Unconventional: Did the bystander say "how are you?"?

Conventional: We asked, "When will the renovations be finished?"

Unconventional: We asked, "When will the renovations be finished?".

Conventional: I yelled, "Look out!"

Unconventional: I yelled, "Look out!".

Conventional: They said, "The renovations will be finished on Friday."

Unconventional: They said, "The renovations will be finished on Friday.".

2. Question marks, exclamation marks, and dashes should displace commas rather than be next to them. Ellipses indicating manner of speech displace commas as well.

Example 203.

Conventional: "What are you doing?" I asked.

Unconventional: "What are you doing?," I asked.

Unconventional: "What are you doing," I asked.

Conventional: "I wonder..." I said.

Unconventional: "I wonder...," I said.

Conventional: "What the —" I said.

Unconventional: "What the —," I said.

3. Don't place dashes next to semicolons, colons, or commas.

Example 204.

Conventional: Bring the following items for your examination — and no, we're not joking: fire extinguisher, top hat, novelty shoes, tomato.

Unconventional: Bring the following items for your examination — and no, we're not joking — : fire extinguisher, top hat, novelty shoes, tomato.

Conventional: The work was completed — amazingly enough — so we took a break.

Unconventional: The work was completed — amazingly enough — , so we took a break.

4. Within a sentence, use terminal punctuation within parentheses or within pairs of dashes only if it is used to indicate manner of speech or, in the case of parentheses, to separate sentences. If multiple sentences are enclosed within parentheses within a sentence, capitalization should occur only after terminal punctuation or for some other logical reason such as preserving the original capitalization of a quotation.

Example 205.

1. We finished the repairs — can you believe it? — so we took a break.

   Remark. Terminal punctuation appears within dashes to indicate manner of speech.

2. We finished the repairs (finally!), so we took a break.

   Remark. Terminal punctuation appears within parentheses to indicate manner of speech.

3. We finished the repairs — we could hardly believe it — so we took a break.

   Remark. The sentence enclosed within dashes is not an exclamation or question, so no terminal punctuation is needed.

4. We finished the repairs (we could hardly believe it), so we took a break.

   Remark. The sentence enclosed within parentheses is not an exclamation or question, so no terminal punctuation is needed.

5. The work was completed (we could hardly believe it. We were even ahead of schedule), so we took a break.

   Remark. A period is needed to separate multiple sentences enclosed within parentheses. The first sentence does not begin with a capital letter, but the second one does, since it immediately follows terminal punctuation.

6. We finished the repairs. (We could hardly believe it.) We were even ahead of schedule.

   Remark. If it is not nested within another sentence, a parenthetical sentence is capitalized and terminated as usual.

7. I forgot to turn in my report (the professor didn't mind, though).

   Remark. The sentence enclosed within parentheses is not an exclamation or question, so no terminal punctuation is needed. The sentence including the parenthetical material terminates as usual.

8. Why did you forget to turn in your report (did your professor mind?)?

   Remark. Terminal punctuation is used within parentheses to indicate manner of speech. The sentence including the parenthetical material terminates as usual.

5. Do not place a terminal period immediately after an abbreviation that ends in a period.

Example 206.

Conventional: I meant Jr., not Sr.

Unconventional: I meant Jr., not Sr..

Conventional: I bought supplies yesterday (a compass, batteries, a first aid kit, etc.).

We believe our punctuation guidelines will keep you out of trouble and make what you write easier to read. However, punctuation conventions can vary from audience to audience, and not everyone will agree with our recommendations. You should use the conventions your readers are expecting if their conventions differ from ours.

Specialized situations (e.g. source citation) tend to have their own punctuation customs. Look to a manual that applies to your specific situation.

Chapter 3

Diction

An error in diction involves meaning to say one thing but actually saying another. In this chapter, we explore several ways of avoiding this mistake.

3.1 Modifiers

1. Make sure modifiers describe what they are meant to. Don't forget that phrases and clauses can function as modifiers.

Example 207.

1. **Completely repainted**, I took my car for a drive.

   Remark. *Completely repainted* incorrectly modifies the speaker. The intended meaning is "I took my completely repainted car for a drive."

2. **As your doctor**, your health is of great concern to me.

   Remark. *As your doctor* incorrectly modifies *health*. The intended meaning is "as your doctor, I am greatly concerned about your health."

3. **Looking at the beautiful scenery**, my anxiety faded away.

   Remark. The anxiety was not looking at scenery. The intended meaning is "while I was looking at the beautiful scenery, my anxiety faded away."

4. **Thinking about all the problems that they were facing**, their anxiety grew.

   Remark. *Thinking*, despite being closer to the intended noun *they*, illogically modifies *anxiety*. "That they were facing" is a separate clause that modifies *problems*, and "about all the problems that they were facing" is a prepositional phrase that modifies *thinking*; *thinking* does not actually relate to *they* directly. The intended meaning is "their anxiety grew as they thought about all the problems they were facing."

5. You lost my equipment, **which hinders me greatly**.

   Remark. *Equipment* is the only noun that *which hinders me greatly* can modify. The relative clause is actually meant to describe an unstated noun. The intended meaning is "your losing my equipment hinders me greatly."

6. They gave gifts to their friends **that they purchased and wrapped the other day**.

   Remark. The clause "that they purchased and wrapped the other day" incorrectly modifies *friends*. The intended meaning is "to their friends they gave gifts that they purchased and wrapped the other day."

---

7. Happy **belated** <u>birthday</u>.

   Remark. The birthday is not belated; the congratulatory remarks are. *Belated "happy birthday"* is the intended meaning.

8. You were pressing **random** <u>buttons</u>.

   Remark. The buttons are not random. You were pressing buttons **randomly**. That is, *random* describes how you were pressing them, not the buttons themselves.

2. Don't confuse absolute constructions with misused modifiers. Absolute constructions are not errors.

Example 208.

1. The <u>work</u> **having been finished**, we took a break.

   Remark. "Having been finished" modifies *work*. The absolute construction "the work having been finished" modifies the rest of the sentence.

2. **Having been exhausted**, <u>sleep</u> sounded like a good idea.

   Remark. "Having been exhausted" is a misused modifier. The intended meaning is "having been exhausted, I thought sleep sounded like a good idea."

3. **Considering the weather forecast**, the <u>game</u> was postponed.

   Remark. Misused modifiers involving *considering, regarding,* or other words that express generalized mental activity are often considered acceptable. Still, writing "considering the weather forecast, we postponed the game" would be better in this case.

3. *Only, all, almost, just, nearly, merely, not,* and *even* are frequently misplaced. Be especially careful when positioning them in your writing.

Example 209.

1. We only started construction after approval was granted.
   Remark. We started construction but did nothing else.

2. We started construction only after approval was granted.
   Remark. There was no construction before the approval.

3. They all can't be right.
   Remark. Nobody can be right. That is, everyone must be wrong.

4. They can't all be right.
   Remark. Not everyone can be right. That is, at least one person must be wrong.

4. Sometimes, modifiers are just unnecessary and can make you say something unintended or nonsensical.

Example 210.

1. I'll really miss not being able to talk with you.

   Remark. The speaker probably means "I'll really miss being able to talk with you." The modifier *not* significantly changes the meaning expressed.

2. I'm sure you probably just forgot.

   Remark. Say "you probably just forgot" or "I'm sure you just forgot," depending on your intended meaning.

3. We're confident that we might find a solution.

   Remark. Instead, say "we're confident that we will find a solution" or "we might find a solution."

4. Sometimes, I never know what's going on.

   Remark. Instead, say "sometimes, I don't know what's going on" or "I never know what's going on."

5. I can't hardly move.

   Remark. "I can hardly move" is the intended meaning. "I can't move" also works.

6. I hardly never go.

   Remark. Say "I never go" or "I hardly ever go" instead.

7. It will cost trillions of dollars — about $3 trillion to be exact.

   Remark. *About* and *exact* don't make any sense together.

3.2 Nouns

Ensure that each noun expresses your intended meaning.

3.2.1 Subjects

Remember what you're talking about.

Example 211.

1. While attending school, my knowledge increased.

   Remark. "While attending school" should modify the speaker, but the subject is actually *knowledge.* Instead, write "while I was attending school, my knowledge increased."

2. While cooking dinner, my food caught fire.

   Remark. "While cooking dinner" should modify the speaker, but the actual subject is *food.* Instead, write "while I was cooking dinner, my food caught fire."

3. To strike the ball correctly, your eyes must be focused on it.

   Remark. The intended subject is *you*, but the actual subject is *eyes.* Instead, write "to strike the ball correctly, you must focus on it."

4. People that post obscene comments will be deleted.

Remark. "Deleting" people makes no sense. Instead, write "obscene comments will be deleted."

5. The airplane and the control tower did not understand each other.

   Remark. More accurately, the pilot and the air traffic controller did not understand each other.

6. Their religion believes there is only one god.

   Remark. Religions do not believe. The followers of the religion believe.

3.2.2   Pronouns

Ensure that pronouns refer to the right things.

Example 212.   Faulty pronoun reference

1. The players' crucial mistakes occurred when they lost track of what they were doing.

   Remark. Players' is actually a modifier that describes *mistakes. Players,* the intended antecedent, is unstated. As a result, the pronouns incorrectly refer to *mistakes.* Instead, write "when they lost track of what they were doing, the players made crucial mistakes."

2. Suppose that a person's home is remodeled while he is away.

   Remark. Person's, a modifier that describes *home,* can't be the antecedent of *he.* The intended antecedent, *person,* is not mentioned. Instead, write "suppose that while a person is away, his home is remodeled."

3. The roads here were expanded. This has reduced the number of traffic jams.

   Remark. This does not have anything to refer to. "The expansion has reduced..." is better.

4. If we are wrong, which we are not, we will have to pay a fine.

   Remark. Which has nothing to refer to. Instead, write "if we were wrong, we would have to pay a fine." The subjunctive mood expresses the idea that we are not actually wrong.

Careless shifts in person can sometimes result in nonsensical statements. Shift person if you have a good reason; otherwise, be consistent.

Example 213.   Careless shifts in person

1. **One** functions more efficiently when **you're** adequately rested.

   Remark. The sentence actually asserts that people in general function more efficiently when you, the reader, are adequately rested. Instead, say "**one** functions more efficiently when **one** is adequately rested" or "**you** function more efficiently when **you're** adequately rested."

2. You are **somebody** that writes down all **your** thoughts.

   Remark. Are you really some third party (i.e. somebody) that writes down another person's thoughts (in this case, yours)? Change *your* to *his* or *her.*

3. **I** would monitor **your** blood pressure.

   Remark. The sentence actually suggests that a person is going to monitor someone else's blood pressure. The intended meaning is "I suggest that **you** monitor **your** blood pressure."

3.2.3   Collective nouns

Do not ascribe to a collective noun characteristics that belong only to its elements.

Example 214.

Wrong: The audience showed its appreciation by clapping its hands.

Remark. An audience does not have hands. The **people** in the audience have hands.

Right: Those in the audience showed their appreciation by clapping their hands.

Right: The audience showed their appreciation by clapping their hands.

Remark. Plural pronouns implicitly refer to the members of the collective noun.

3.2.4   Number

Check each noun to make sure it is the proper number.

Example 215. Mistakes with number

1. Students that wish to compete should submit an application.

   Remark. Unless all the students will collectively work on a single application, the sentence should read "students that wish to compete should submit applications" or "each student that wishes to compete should submit an application."

2. Both were allowed admission despite not having a ticket.

   Remark. Can a ticket be shared by several people? If not, the sentence should read "both were allowed admission despite not having tickets" or "each was allowed admission despite not having a ticket."

3.3   Comparisons

Make sure the things you're trying to compare really are comparable. Usually, a comparison will involve a word such as *like, unlike, than,* or *as.*

Example 216.

1. Wrong: The Pacific Ocean is larger than any body of water on earth.

   Remark. The Pacific Ocean is a body of water on Earth and cannot be larger than itself.

2. Right: The Pacific Ocean is larger than any other body of water on earth.

3. Wrong: Our latest program is faster than any other previous version of it.

   Remark. The latest program is not a previous version of itself.

4. Right: Our latest program is faster than any previous version of it.

5. Wrong: They are more experienced than anyone.

6. Right: They are more experienced than anyone else.

7. Wrong: My presentation was longer than anyone else.

   Remark. The presentation is not longer than a person. It is longer than other presentations.

8. Right: My presentation was longer than anyone else's.

9. Wrong: The function of a saw is different from a hammer.

10. Right: The function of a saw is different from that of a hammer.

11. Wrong: A saw's function is different from a hammer.

12. Right: A saw's function is different from a hammer's.

13. Wrong: The grade I received was relative to the other students taking the examination.

14. Right: The grade I received was relative to the grades of the other students taking the examination.

15. Wrong: My shoes are bigger than my friend.

    Remark. The shoes are bigger than a person?

16. Right: My shoes are bigger than those of my friend.

17. Right: My shoes are bigger than my friend's shoes.

18. Right: My shoes are bigger than my friend's.

19. Wrong: Unlike in our first attempt, we did not make any mistakes.

20. Wrong: Unlike our first attempt, we did not make any mistakes.

21. Right: Unlike our first attempt, our second attempt did not contain any mistakes.

22. Wrong: No sooner had I fallen asleep when my alarm clock rang.

    Remark. The sentence attempts to compare the timing of two events but fails to answer the question "sooner than what?" Some rearranging makes the incomplete comparison easier to see: "I had fallen asleep no sooner when my alarm clock rang" makes no sense. Clearly, *when* is the wrong word. One event occurs "no sooner than another," not "no sooner when another."

23. Right: No sooner had I fallen asleep than my alarm clock rang.

24. Right: Barely had I fallen asleep when my alarm clock rang.

    Remark. Removing the word *sooner* eliminates the comparison, so *than* is not needed.

3.4   Omissions

When omitting words, ensure that:

1. The reader can easily determine what has been omitted.

2. The reader can immediately recognize the existence of the omission.

3. The omission does not cause awkwardness or misreading.

4. You are not forcing one expression to serve more than one grammatical role.

5. No errors result from filling in the expected missing words.

Example 217. Poor omissions

1. I like pizza more than my friend.

   Remark. The sentence could mean "I like pizza more than my friend likes pizza" or "I like pizza more than I like my friend."

2. My friend has faced more skilled competitors than I.

   Remark. The sentence could be about facing "more skilled competitors than I have" or "competitors more skilled than I am."

3. The consensus is overwhelming thunderstorms will result.

   Remark. The sentence could mean "the consensus is overwhelming that thunderstorms will result" or "the consensus is that overwhelming thunderstorms will result."

4. We read parts of the *Iliad* and the *Odyssey*.

   Remark. Whether "parts of" has been omitted before "the *Odyssey*" is unclear. Say "parts of the *Iliad* and parts of the *Odyssey*" or "the *Odyssey* and parts of the *Iliad*."

5. We expect the average to fall between one and three hundred.

   Remark. "One" could actually stand for "one hundred." The reader can't be sure.

6. If it seems too good to be true, it probably is.

   Remark. Either "too good to be true" or "true" could follow *is.* "If it seems too good to be true, it's probably false" is clearer.

Do not omit *that* before a clause it normally introduces if the omission obscures the presence of the clause.

Example 218.

1. Awkward: We are concerned they are behind schedule.
2. Better: We are concerned **that** they are behind schedule.
3. Awkward: The notion they are responsible for this is unfounded.
4. Better: The notion **that** they are responsible for this is unfounded.
5. Acceptable: I said they would be late.
6. Acceptable: I think they already left.
7. Acceptable: This is the book I was talking about.

Omitting *that* before a phrase functioning as an object may incorrectly make part of the phrase appear to be the object instead. Often, a verb such as *acknowledge, believe,* or *report* is involved.

Example 219.

1. Awkward: The researchers reported half of their results have been confirmed so far.

2. Better: The researchers reported **that** half of their results have been confirmed so far.

3. Awkward: The government has confirmed the news report is false.

4. Better: The government has confirmed **that** the news report is false.

5. Awkward: While acknowledging criticism has been exaggerated, they still propose the new treatment be tested further.

6. Better: While acknowledging **that** criticism has been exaggerated, they still propose **that** the new treatment be tested further.

7. Awkward: They believe their relatives are doing well.

8. Better: They believe **that** their relatives are doing well.

Make sure leaving out a subject does not cause any confusion.

Example 220. A confusing omission

I assumed you had proofread the documents and submitted them.

Remark. The sentence could mean "I assumed you had proofread the documents, and I submitted them" or "I assumed that you had proofread and submitted the documents."

Often, omitting something from the first phrase(s) of a series causes problems because the reader expects the omitted words to be stated exactly in the final phrase.

Example 221. In each wrong example, the bold words are understood to follow each bracketed phrase.

1. Wrong: Our giant flag is <as big> or <bigger than> **Antarctica**.

   Remark. The implied omission is "Antarctica," but "as Antarctica" has been omitted. Supplying the implied omission results in the flawed statement "our giant flag is as big Antarctica or bigger than Antarctica."

2. Right: Our giant flag is as big as or bigger than Antarctica.

3. Wrong: I <have not yet> but <will eventually> **study**.

   Remark. The complete statement is apparently "I have not yet study but will eventually study."

4. Right: I have not yet studied but will eventually study.

5. Wrong: Everyone is either <opposed> or <in favor of> **our proposal**.

6. Right: Everyone is either opposed to or in favor of our proposal.

7. Wrong: I do not know why we are even <considering>, <let alone hoping>, **for a root canal**.

   Remark. Filling in the implied omission, "for a root canal," results in "I do not know why we are even considering for a root canal, let alone hoping for a root canal."

8. Right: I do not know why we are even considering, let alone hoping for, a root canal.

9. Wrong: It is <one of the best>, <if not the best>, **book I have read**.

   Remark. The complete sentence would be "it is one of the best book I have read, if not the best book I have read."

10. Right: It is one of the best books, if not the best book, I have read.

11. Wrong: <The school may> — <and occasionally has> — **changed its graduation requirements**.
12. Right: The school may change — and occasionally has changed — its graduation requirements.
13. Wrong: We <wrote>, <edited>, and <sent> **our essays to the publisher.**
14. Right: We wrote and edited our essays and sent them to the publisher.

However, omission is usually permissible in the final phrase.

Example 222.

Wrong: Our giant flag is as big, if not bigger than Antarctica.

Right: Our giant flag is as big as Antarctica, if not bigger.

Avoid using a single expression to serve several different grammatical roles. The shift in grammatical function is often awkward.

Example 223.

1. Wrong: They are present and creating a lot of commotion.
   Remark. *Are* is used as a linking verb and as an auxiliary. Instead, write "they are present and are creating a lot of commotion."

2. Wrong: Pursue what you love and benefits society.
   Remark. *What* is the object of *love* and the subject of *benefits*. Instead, write "pursue what you love and what benefits society."

3. Wrong: Here are the rules that keep everyone safe and you must follow.
   Remark. *That* is the object of *follow* and the subject of *keep*. Instead, write "here are the rules that keep everyone safe and that you must follow."

4. Wrong: They were skilled and chosen for the job.
5. Right: They were skilled and were chosen for the job.
6. Wrong: The castle was an impressive building, the rooms of which we were in awe.
7. Right: The castle was an impressive building, the rooms of which we were in awe of.

A lot of people will omit the final *of* in sentence 7 of example 223 because they think the preposition is superfluous. The sentence is clumsy, but it is correct; some rearranging makes the error of the omission clear. Consider the second half of the correct sentence:

The rooms of which we were in awe of.

Place *the rooms of which* at the end:

We were in awe of the rooms of which.

Replace *which* with its antecedent:

We were in awe of the rooms of the castle.

Now, you can easily see that neither *of* should be omitted.

Example 224. Determining the necessity of a preposition

Wrong: The building was a castle of which we were in awe of.

Right: The building was a castle of which we were in awe.

Wrong: You are my friend, in whom I have trusted my secrets in.

Right: You are my friend, in whom I have trusted my secrets.

Wrong: Questions are addressed in the order they are received.

Right: Questions are addressed in the order they are received in.

The best way to determine correct usage is to think about the structure of your sentence. For example, consider the sentence "questions are addressed in the order they are received in." *Order* is the complement of the first *in*. "In the order" is a prepositional phrase that modifies the verb *are addressed*. "They are received in" modifies *order*. The object of the second *in* is actually an implied relative pronoun, *which*. The antecedent of the implied *which* is *order*.

An equivalent phrasing would be "questions are addressed in the order in which they are received." To see how, move the second *in* to the end:

Questions are addressed in the order which they are received in.

Finally, make the relative pronoun *which* implied (i.e. leave it out):

Questions are addressed in the order they are received in.

3.5   Using expressions properly

Nothing damages your credibility as a writer like misusing an expression. Incorrectly using a word or phrase is sure to make you appear ignorant, pretentious, or careless.

This section presents several guidelines for avoiding erroneous vocabulary, along with some examples of frequently misused words and phrases. For a list of commonly misused expressions, see the appendix.

3.5.1   Don't abuse technical language.

Specialized terminology does occasionally take on more general meanings, but if you don't want to risk being branded as uneducated, you should use technical language in its technical sense. Besides, unnecessarily using unfamiliar jargon can only hamper your ability to communicate clearly. Look for simpler, clearer ways of expressing yourself, and avoid technical terms if there is no need for them.

quantum leap   A quantum leap is a discontinuous change from one state to another. Many people use the expression to mean "a large change," but quantum leaps don't have to be large. Actually, the expression is used to describe how an electron changes from one energy level to another.

epicenter   An epicenter is the point on the Earth's surface directly above an earthquake's point of origin. Don't say that some place is "the epicenter of the economy." That doesn't make any sense.

bandwidth   Bandwidth is the transmission capacity of a communication system. Saying something like "I have the bandwidth to sprint for three hours" is ridiculous. Say *capacity* or *ability* instead.

schizophrenia   Schizophrenia is a mental disorder often characterized by hallucinations, delusions, behavioral disturbances, social isolation, and intellectual deterioration. Do not confuse the condition with "multiple personality disorder" or "dissociative identity disorder."

paranoid   Paranoia is characterized by extreme, irrational mistrust of others. To say you are paranoid is to say you are unjustifiably fearful. Do not use "paranoid" simply to mean "very afraid."

order of magnitude   Order of magnitude can be roughly thought of as the smallest power of 10 needed to represent some quantity (assuming no other base is specified). Don't use "by an order of magnitude" simply to mean "by a large amount"; an order of magnitude difference is a difference of a particular size. For example, 1000 is greater than 100 by one order of magnitude. To say something is "orders of magnitude" greater is to say that it is at least 100 times greater.

Law of Large Numbers   The Law of Large Numbers is a theorem that characterizes the convergence of a sample statistic to its theoretical value. Some inappropriately use the term to describe the idea that corporations have more difficulty growing as they get larger. The Law of Large Numbers applies to repeated, independent occurrences of a random event (e.g. flipping a coin 10 million times). The theorem has nothing to do with slowing profit growth.

exponential   Something grows exponentially if the rate at which it increases is proportional to its size. Populations often grow exponentially, for instance. Some people describe very rapid but constant growth as "exponential," but mathematicians don't, and you shouldn't either. Also, don't bother with questionable expressions such as "exponentially more important" when so many sound alternatives exist (e.g. *vastly more important, significantly more important, drastically more important*).

We once heard a person on television really mess up while he was commenting on a political candidate's increasing popularity. We imagine he meant to say that the popularity was "growing exponentially," but he said "growing logarithmically" instead. Something that grows logarithmically increases more slowly as it progresses, so he actually said the opposite of what he meant to. It's sad, but he didn't even misuse the right word.

bug, insect   *Bug* and *insect* are not interchangeable terms. A bug is a specific type of insect (i.e. not all insects are bugs). Spiders, ticks, scorpions, and mites are not insects, by the way. They're arachnids.

stomach   *Stomach* is the name of a particular digestive organ. Don't use the term as a synonym for *abdomen* or *belly.*

instinct   Instinct is innate (i.e. inborn rather than learned). Don't say something like "people can form sentences by instinct." Humans must learn how to speak and write. They may eventually be able to construct sentences "intuitively" or "unconsciously," but they cannot do so "instinctively."

3.5.2   Don't be fooled by appearance.

Consult a dictionary if you aren't completely sure about the definition of an expression. Don't try to guess what the meaning might be — words don't always mean what they appear to mean.

obsolescent   It doesn't mean "obsolete." It means "becoming obsolete."

noisome   It has nothing to do with sound. It means "having an exceptionally offensive smell."

fortuitous   It doesn't mean "fortunate." It means "happening by chance." Something tragic can be fortuitous.

idyllic   It means *charmingly simple*, not *ideal.*

gratuitous   It's not the adjective form of "gratitude." It means "unwarranted" or "done without reason."

suffrage   It has nothing to do with suffering. Suffrage is the right to vote.

peruse   It doesn't mean *skim*. To peruse is to read carefully.

restive   It means *nervously impatient* or *restless*.

3.5.3   Be careful when forming different parts of speech.

If you need to turn a particular word into a different part of speech and aren't sure how, consult a dictionary.

conversation   The verb is *converse*, not *conversate*.

paralyze   The noun is *paralysis*, not *paralyzation*.

genius   It's a noun, not a modifier. Don't say "a genius plan." Say "a brilliant plan."

Admittedly, these first three restrictions don't appear to serve any purpose. There is no particular reason that *genius* can't be a modifier or that *paralysis* must be the only nominal form of *paralyze*. Sometimes, though, getting the form wrong actually changes your meaning (see the next entries), so be careful.

emergent   This word isn't related to *emergency*. "Emergent" is the adjectival form of *emerge*, which means "to come into existence" or "to become visible." *Emergent supplies* doesn't make any sense. Say *emergency supplies*.

enormous   Use *enormousness* as the nominal form. Don't use *enormity*, since it can also mean "a serious crime."

3.5.4   Examine the construction of a word.

We don't particularly care about whether the *t* in *often* is silent or whether *schism* is pronounced *skiz-um*, *siz-um*, or *shiz-um*. However, some pronunciation errors show that you simply weren't paying attention. Almost all the mispronunciations detailed below are indefensible if you examine the spelling of the word.

1. *adultery* (*uh-dul-tur-ee*) not *adult-tree* or *adult-chur-ee*
2. *epitome* (*e-pit-oh-me*) not *eh-pih-tome*
3. *grievous* (*gree-vuhs*) not *gree-vee-uhs*
4. *height* (rhymes with fight) no -*th* sound at the end
5. *relevant* (*rel-eh-vant*) not *rev-eh-lant*
6. *jewelry* (*jew-wel-ree*) not *jew-ler-ee*
7. *library* (*lie-brare-ee*) not *lie-berry*
8. *mischievous* (*mis-ch-vus*) not *mis-chee-vee-us*
9. *nuclear* (*new-clee-ur*) not *new-cue-lar*
10. *peripheral* (*per-if-er-al*) not *per-rif-free-al*
11. *probably* (*prah-bah-bly*) not *prob-ly*
12. *prodigy* (*prah-dih-gee*) not *prah-gih-dee*
13. *resonate* (*res-oh-nait*) not *reh-sig-nate*
14. *tentative* (*ten-tah-tiv*) not *ten-uh-tiv*
15. *tragedy* (*tra-juh-dee*) not *tra-duh-gee*

3.5.5   Don't slur.

1. Use *going to*, not *gonna*.
2. Use *got to*, not *gotta*.
3. Use *got you*, not *gotcha*.
4. Use *want to*, not *wanna*.

3.5.6 Don't change an expression unnecessarily.

realm of possibility   Don't make *realm* plural. The realm of possibility, by definition, encompasses everything that is possible. *Realms of possibility* makes no sense. There is only one realm of possibility.

somewhere   Occasionally written incorrectly as *somewheres*. Adding the *s* doesn't accomplish anything.

anyway   Adding an *s* to form *anyways* accomplishes nothing.

a way to go   There is no point in making *way* plural, as in *they have a ways to go*. You shouldn't use *a* with plural nouns, anyway.

in regard to   Don't say *in regards to*. Leave *regard* singular or say *regarding*.

regardless   *Irregardless* is a senseless term. The prefix accomplishes nothing.

plan   Don't use *pre-plan* to mean *plan*. *Plan* already means itself. Don't say that you are "pre-planning an event" if you mean that you are "planning an event."

thus   Adding *-ly* to form *thusly* is pointless. *Thus* is already an adverb.

thaw   Sometimes, people meaning to write *thaw* will write *unthaw*. To thaw is to soften by warming up. *Unthaw* would logically be synonymous with *freeze*.

3.5.7 Make sense of an expression.

3.5.7.1 Mentally expand abbreviations such as contractions and acronyms.

ISBN, PIN   In both acronyms, the *N* stands for *number*. "PIN number" is redundant.

RSVP   *RSVP* stands for a French phrase meaning "please reply," so don't write "please RSVP." Better yet, don't use French for no reason.

there's   *There's* stands for *there is* and should not be used with plural subjects. Do not say "there's several things to resolve." No one would say "there is things to resolve."

aren't   "Aren't I?" is a common construction, but it is short for "I are not," which is obviously wrong.

it's | its   *It's* stands for *it is*; *its* is a possessive pronoun.

we're | were   *We're* stands for "we are." *Were* is a verb.

Example 225.

1. Wrong: Read it's introduction.
   Remark. Expanding the contraction results in "read it is introduction," which makes no sense.

2. Right: Read its introduction.
3. Wrong: Its an entertaining book.
4. Right: It's an entertaining book.
   Remark. "It is an entertaining book" makes sense.

5. Wrong: You we're right.
   Remark. "You we are right" makes no sense.

6. Right: You were right.

3.5.7.2   Question illogical expressions.

all for naught (illogical: all for not, all for knot)   *Naught* is an archaic word that means *nothing*. "All for naught" means "all for nothing."

could have (illogical: could of)   *Could have* is a verb containing the auxiliary *could*. "Could of" (an auxiliary and a preposition) makes no sense. *Would of, must of,* and *should of* are also errors.

with all due respect (illogical: with all do respect, with all-do respect)   Something due is owed, deserved, expected, or required (e.g. a payment due at the end of the month). When you say something with all due respect, you say it giving the listeners all the respect they deserve.

reap what you sow (illogical: reap what you sew)   *Reap* means *gather* or *harvest.* To sow is to plant seeds.

wreaking havoc (illogical: reeking havoc, wrecking havoc)   To wreak is to cause or to inflict. To reek is to give off an offensive smell. To wreck is to destroy.

rite of passage (illogical: right of passage)   A rite is a ceremony. A rite of passage is an occasion that marks an important moment in a person's life. Of course, you can say "right of passage" if you mean "entitlement to pass."

shudder to think (illogical: shutter to think)   To shudder is to tremble from fear or excitement. If you shudder to think something, then thinking about it makes you shake with emotion. A *shutter* is a hinged window blind or part of a camera.

straitjacket (illogical: straightjacket)   *Strait* refers to a narrow passage of water (as in *Bering Strait*) or to a difficult situation (as in *dire straits*). A straitjacket is a garment designed to make movement difficult. The name relates to something constrictive and troublesome, not to something that isn't crooked.

statute of limitations (illogical: statue of limitations)   A statute is a rule. Generally, a statute of limitations restricts the amount of time a person may wait before taking legal action. No sculpting is involved.

supposed to (illogical: suppose to), opposed to (illogical: oppose to)   To suppose is to think or assume. Something that is supposed is thought or assumed; something supposed to be the best is thought to be the best. You wouldn't say "it is think to be the best," so don't say "it is suppose to be the best."

To oppose is to resist. Someone that opposes you is opposed to you.

Similar errors are often made with *bias* and *prejudice*. "A bias judge" is incorrect. The phrase should be "a biased judge." *Bias* and *prejudice* are either nouns or verbs — not adjectives. Saying "a prejudice judge" is like saying "a polish floor." The correct expressions are "a prejudiced judge" and "a polished floor."

woe is me (illogical: whoa is me)   *Woe* is another word for *distress*, and *woe is me* is an expression of anxiety. *Whoa* is a command to stop or slow down.

self-esteem (illogical: self-steam)   *Esteem* is synonymous with *respect.* Another term for *self-respect* is *self-esteem.*

Other mistakes include:

- writing *another words* when you actually mean *in other words*
- writing *cease the day* when you actually mean *seize the day*
- writing *fine toothcomb* when you actually mean *fine-tooth comb*
- writing *for all intensive purposes* when you actually mean *for all intents and purposes*
- writing *minus well* when you actually mean *might as well*
- writing *pause for concern* when you actually mean *cause for concern*
- writing *point of you* when you actually mean *point of view*
- writing *pre-madonna* when you actually mean *prima donna*

- writing *readably available* when you actually mean *readily available*
- writing *signaled out* when you actually mean *singled out*
- writing *slight of hand* when you actually mean *sleight of hand*
- writing *strike a cord* when you actually mean *strike a chord*

3.5.7.3   Think about whether words should be joined.

a lot   This expression consists of the article *a* and the noun *lot*, which means *group* or *set*. A lot of apples is a group of apples. Joining the terms (i.e. *alot*) doesn't make any sense, just as joining *a* and *group* doesn't make any sense.

apart | a part   *Apart* is an adverb (e.g. *take something apart*). *A part* is a phrase consisting of an article and a noun (e.g. *a part of me is unsure*).

apiece | a piece   *Apiece* is an adverb meaning "to, for, or by each one" (e.g. *the diamonds cost $10,000 apiece*). *A piece* consists of an article and a noun (e.g. *a piece of paper*).

anyone | any one   *Anyone* is a pronoun (e.g. *anyone can participate*). *Any one* means "any single entity" (e.g. *any one of the words might be misspelled*).

anyway | any way   *Anyway* is an adverb (e.g. *we're not sure, but we'll try anyway*). *Any way* consists of a modifier and a noun (e.g. *is there any way to solve the problem?*).

away | a way   *Away* is a modifier (e.g. *walk away; go away*). *A way* consists of an article and a noun (e.g. *there is a way to succeed*).

awhile | a while   *Awhile* is an adverb meaning "for a short time" (e.g. *stay there awhile*). *A while* consists of an article and the noun *while*, which means "a period of time" (e.g. *stay for a while*).

everyday | every day   *Everyday* is an adjective meaning *ordinary* (e.g. *everyday clothing*). *Every day* means "each day" (e.g. *we train every day; we make the most of every day*).

everyone | every one   *Everyone* is a pronoun meaning "all the people" (e.g. *everyone loves a good story*). *Every one*, consisting of an adjective and a noun, means "each one" (e.g. *every one of you*).

every time   *Every time* means *each time* and should be two words, just as *each time* is.

in-depth | in depth   *In-depth* is an adjective (e.g. *an in-depth report*). *In depth* is a prepositional phrase used as an adverb (e.g. *study the material in depth*).

in fact   *In fact* is just like any other prepositional phrase. Don't run the words together.

into | in to   *Into* is a preposition that addresses the question "where" (e.g. *we went into the building*). The "where" doesn't have to be an actual place (e.g. *I went into a trance; I went into business*). *In to* consists of an adverb and a preposition. For example, in the sentence "I went in to lie down," *in* modifies *went*.

"I turned my assignment into the teacher" means that I magically transformed the assignment into a person. "I turned my assignment in to the teacher" means I submitted the assignment to be graded.

maybe | may be   *Maybe* is an adverb (e.g. *maybe we will be early*). *May be* is a verb that includes the auxiliary *may* (e.g. *it may be our only hope*).

onto | on to   *Onto* is a preposition (e.g. *we ran onto the stage*). *On to* consists of an adverb and a preposition. For example, in the sentence "hold on to the rope," *on* modifies *hold*.

"We walked onto the field" means that we began walking on the field. "We walked on to the field" means we continued walking toward the field.

sometime | some time   *Sometime* means "at some time" (e.g. *I will see you again sometime*). *Some time* consists of a modifier and a noun (e.g. *I saved some time by taking a shortcut*).

Be careful with verb-adverb combinations (especially if the adverb looks like a preposition). If joining the verb and its adverb is possible, doing so will result in a noun or an adjective. You can join terms by running them together or by using a hyphen.

Example 226.

1. blow up | blow-up | blowup

    (a) Blow up a balloon.
    (b) This is a blow-up raft.
    (c) We have a blowup of the photograph.

2. break down | breakdown

    (a) This machine might break down.
    (b) This machine might have a breakdown.

3. clean up | cleanup

    (a) Clean up this room.
    (b) The cleanup is nearly finished.

4. lift off | liftoff

    (a) The airplane is about to lift off.
    (b) Prepare for liftoff.

5. make up | make-up | makeup

    (a) Make up a story.
    (b) Take a make-up examination.
    (c) Don't put on any makeup.

6. mix up | mixup

    (a) Don't mix up these two words.
    (b) There has been a mixup.

7. warm up | warm-up | warmup

    (a) Warm up before you start.
    (b) Perform some warm-up exercises.
    (c) Perform a warmup before you exercise.

3.5.8 Pay careful attention to expressions that define relationships.

Make sure you explain relationships correctly. Doing so is usually a matter of carefully selecting prepositions and conjunctions, though you should keep in mind that modifiers often express relationships as well.

substitute with | substitute for   To substitute apples **with** oranges is to replace apples with oranges. To substitute apples **for** oranges is to replace oranges with apples.

graduate | graduate from   Students graduate **from** a school. A school graduates students. Students do not "graduate school."

wait on | wait for   To wait **on** is to serve. The person that brings you food in a restaurant waits on you. To wait **for** is to remain until a particular condition is met. You are not tired of waiting **on** someone to show up. You are tired of waiting **for** someone to show up.

onto | on   *On* can sometimes take the place of *onto* without any problem (e.g. *it fell on the ground*). Other times, replacing *onto* with *on* can cause confusion. "Throw the ball on the table" could mean "throw the ball that is on the table," "throw the ball onto the table," or "throw the ball while you are on the table."

Example 227. Expressing relationships poorly

1. The company prevailed over all its competitors and then became the most dominant corporation in its industry.

    Remark. The adverb *then* implies that "prevailing over competitors" and "becoming dominant" were different events, when in fact they are two descriptions of the same occurrence.

2. I donated a lot of money to charities last year, while my friend did the same.

   Remark. *And* better clarifies the relationship. *While* means *at the same time* or *although* but is frequently used where *and* is more appropriate.

3.5.9 Using auxiliaries properly

3.5.9.1 may | might

May and *might* can express permission or possibility. Generally, most people use *may* and *might* interchangeably, though some reserve *may* for present possibilities and *might* for possibilities that used to exist but no longer do. We recommend using *may* (instead of *might*) to express permission.

Example 228.

1. Possibility

   (a) I may go for a walk tomorrow. Yesterday, I might have gone, but I was too busy.
   (b) This new medicine may have helped.
       Remark. The medicine's effectiveness is still being determined.
   (c) This new medicine might have helped.
       Remark. The medicine was never taken.

2. Permission

   (a) May I suggest something?
   (b) You may go.

3.5.9.2 can | could

Can and *could* are used to express ability or possibility. *Can* refers to the non-past. *Could* can refer to both the past and the non-past.

Example 229.

1. None of them can run as fast as I could when I was younger.
2. I did not study as much as I could have.
3. I suppose I could study now.
4. I suppose I can study now.
5. I suppose I could study tomorrow.
6. I suppose I can study tomorrow.

People disagree on whether expressing permission with *can* is acceptable. We recommend using *may* instead of *can* for expressing permission, since no one will fault you for doing so.

Example 230.

1. Can you think of a better plan?
2. May I read this book?
3. I don't know whether we can finish in time.
4. You may go now.

3.5.9.3   shall | will

Shall and *will* are most commonly used to refer to future time. They can also express volition, prediction, or determination.

Shall can be used to express offers (e.g. *shall we go?*). When used in second or third person, *shall* implies a command or an obligation (e.g. *you shall not steal*).

Example 231.

1. I shall return.
2. I will be back tomorrow morning.
3. Shall I proceed?
4. This technology will revolutionize medical treatment.
5. So it shall be.

Shall is traditionally thought of as the appropriate form of *will* when using first person, but few observe the distinction now.

3.5.9.4   could, might, should, would

Could, might, should, and *would* can function as the past forms of *can, may, shall,* and *will,* respectively. These "past" auxiliaries are also the appropriate forms to use when referring to hypothetical situations.

Example 232.

1. My equipment broke, and I could not tell where I was.
2. I wondered whether I would make it in time.
3. If we had arrived earlier, we might have been better prepared.
4. If we had arrived earlier, we could have been better prepared.
5. If we had arrived earlier, we would have been better prepared.
6. We should have tried something else.

Could, might, should, and *would* can also refer to non-past time. They can express a wide range of meanings, such as possibility, volition, obligation, and prediction.

Example 233.

1. Tomorrow, I could order soup, or I could order a sandwich.
2. This could be a great opportunity.
3. I might study abroad next year.
4. I should clean up before my guests arrive.
5. This should last us for the rest of the week.
6. Would you help me with my project next week?

Would can express habitual or repeated actions. When habit or repetition is already expressed, using *would* is unnecessary.

Example 234.

Wordy: They would go hiking every weekend.

Better: They went hiking every weekend.

Wordy: Once a year, they would travel abroad.

Better: Once a year, they traveled abroad.

3.5.9.5   Unintentional or illogical use of auxiliaries

Example 235.

1. There is a possibility this may work in your favor.

   Remark. The sentence is actually about the possibility of the possibility of something working in your favor. Instead, say "there is a possibility this will work in your favor" or "this may work in your favor."

2. We're confident that we might find a solution.

   Remark. We are actually expressing our confidence that the odds of finding a solution are greater than zero, rather than that the odds are high. Say "we are confident that we will find a solution," if that's what you mean.

3. Your opponents cannot be underestimated.

   Remark. If your opponents cannot be underestimated, then no opinion is too low, and they are in fact terrible. If you mean to warn people against underestimating them, then say "they should not be underestimated" or "they are not to be underestimated."

4. I might could go.

   Remark. Eliminate *might* or *could* depending on what you mean to say.

3.6 Diction summary

English is always changing, so some of the distinctions we make may not be observed many years from now. Regardless of how the language evolves, you should be fine as long as you abide by the following principles.

Check a dictionary.   Before using an expression, know how to use it correctly. Pay careful attention to an expression's definition, spelling, and pronunciation.

And by "know how to use it" we don't mean "be reasonably confident about how to use it." We mean be absolutely, positively certain that you know. You should look something up if you're not familiar with its dictionary entry, even if you think you know what it means.

Consider the relationships between expressions.   Determine what each modifier describes and what each pronoun represents. Think about the structure of every sentence. What are the subjects? Do the verbs paired with them make sense?

Ask yourself whether you correctly expressed your intended meaning.   After you've crafted a sentence, think for a moment about what it actually says. Does it say what you wanted it to? Pay close attention to comparisons and omissions, as well as to words that express relationships.

Appendix A

Supplements

A.1 Spelling guidelines

1. Forming plurals

   (a) If the noun ends in *s, x, z, sh,* or *ch,* add *-es* (e.g. *boxes, recesses, bushes, patches*).
   (b) If a common noun ends in a consonant followed by *y,* change the *y* to *i* before adding *-es* (e.g. *mysteries*).
   (c) Consult a dictionary when forming the plural of a noun ending in *o, f,* or *fe,* as there are no rules about whether the plural ends in *s* or *es*. Sometimes, to form the plural of a noun ending in *f* or *fe,* you must change the *f* to a *v* (e.g. *leaves, lives*). However, the change is not required of all nouns ending in *f* or *fe* (e.g. *beliefs, safes, roofs*).
   (d) If none of the above guidelines apply, the plural is usually formed by adding *-s* (e.g. *valleys, books*).

2. Forming comparatives and superlatives

   (a) If the modifier (1) is monosyllabic and (2) ends with a vowel followed by a consonant, double the consonant before adding the suffix (e.g. *thinner, thinnest*).
   (b) If the modifier ends with a consonant followed by *y,* change the *y* to *i* before adding *-er* or *-est* (e.g. *happier, happiest*).
   (c) If the modifier ends with a consonant followed by *e,* delete the *e* before adding a suffix (e.g. *later, latest*).

3. Forming participles

   (a) If the verb (1) is monosyllabic and (2) ends with a vowel followed by a consonant, double the consonant before adding the suffix (e.g. *stopping, stopped*).
   (b) If the verb ends with a consonant followed by *y,* change the *y* to *i* before adding *-ed* (e.g. *tried, fried*).
   (c) If the verb ends with a consonant followed by *e,* delete the *e* before adding a suffix (e.g. *comparing, compared, preparing, prepared*). *Being* is an exception.

A.2 Verb forms

Base form	Past form	Past participle
be	was/were	been
bear	bore	born

beat	beat	beaten
beget	begot	begotten
begin	began	begun
bend	bent	bent
bet	bet	bet
bid (offer)	bid	bid
bid (utter)	bade	bidden
bind	bound	bound
bite	bit	bitten
bleed	bled	bled
blow	blew	blown
break	broke	broken
breed	bred	bred
bring	brought	brought
broadcast	broadcast	broadcast
build	built	built
burn	burnt, burned	burnt, burned
burst	burst	burst
bust	bust	bust
buy	bought	bought
can	could	
cast	cast	cast
catch	caught	caught
choose	chose	chosen
cling	clung	clung
clothe	clothed, clad	clothed, clad
come	came	come
cost	cost	cost
creep	crept	crept
cut	cut	cut
deal	dealt	dealt
dig	dug	dug
dive	dived	dived
do	did	done
draw	drew	drawn
dream	dreamt, dreamed	dreamt, dreamed
drink	drank	drunk
drive	drove	driven
eat	ate	eaten
fall	fell	fallen
feed	fed	fed
feel	felt	felt
fight	fought	fought
find	found	found
flee	fled	fled
fling	flung	flung
fly	flew	flown

forbid	forbade	forbidden
forsake	forsook	forsaken
freeze	froze	frozen
get	got	got, gotten
give	gave	given
go	went	gone
grind	ground	ground
grow	grew	grown
hang	hung	hung
hang (execution)	hanged	hanged
have	had	had
hear	heard	heard
hide	hid	hidden
hit	hit	hit
hold	held	held
hurt	hurt	hurt
keep	kept	kept
kneel	knelt	knelt
know	knew	known
lay	laid	laid
lead	led	led
learn	learned	learned
leave	left	left
lend	lent	lent
let	let	let
lie	lay	lain
light	lit	lit
lose	lost	lost
make	made	made
may	might	
mean	meant	meant
meet	met	met
melt	melted	melted, molten
mislead	misled	misled
mow	mowed	mown
pay	paid	paid
plead	pled, pleaded	pled, pleaded
prove	proved	proven
put	put	put
quit	quit	quit
read	read	read
rend	rent	rent
rid	rid	rid
ride	rode	ridden
ring	rang	rung
rise	rose	risen
run	ran	run

saw	sawed	sawn
say	said	said
see	saw	seen
seek	sought	sought
sell	sold	sold
send	sent	sent
set	set	set
sew	sewed	sewn
shake	shook	shaken
shed	shed	shed
shoot	shot	shot
show	showed	shown
shrink	shrank	shrunk
shut	shut	shut
sing	sang	sung
sink	sank	sunk
sit	sat	sat
slay	slew	slain
sleep	slept	slept
slide	slid	slid
sling	slung	slung
slit	slit	slit
smell	smelled	smelled
smite	smote	smitten
sneak	snuck	snuck
sow	sowed	sown
speak	spoke	spoken
speed	sped	sped
spend	spent	spent
spill	spilled	spilled
spin	spun	spun
spit	spat	spat
split	split	split
spoil	spoiled	spoiled
spread	spread	spread
spring	sprang	sprung
stand	stood	stood
steal	stole	stolen
stick	stuck	stuck
sting	stung	stung
stink	stank	stunk
stride	strode	stridden
strike	struck	struck
string	strung	strung
strip	stripped	stripped
strive	strove	striven
sublet	sublet	sublet

swear	swore	sworn
sweat	sweated	sweated
sweep	swept	swept
swell	swelled	swollen
swim	swam	swum
swing	swung	swung
take	took	taken
teach	taught	taught
tear	tore	torn
tell	told	told
think	thought	thought
thrive	thrived	thrived
throw	threw	thrown
thrust	thrust	thrust
tread	trod	trodden
undergo	underwent	undergone
understand	understood	understood
undertake	undertook	undertaken
upset	upset	upset
wake	woke	woken
wear	wore	worn
weave	wove	woven
weep	wept	wept
win	won	won
wind	wound	wound
withdraw	withdrew	withdrawn
withhold	withheld	withheld
withstand	withstood	withstood
wring	wrung	wrung
write	wrote	written

A.3 Commonly misused expressions

Expressions	Comments
a lot, a little	Each expression consists of two words — an article and a noun. Never write either expression as one word. Also, don't confuse "a lot" with "allot," which means "apportion" or "allocate."
absence | lack	absence (noun) failure to be present lack (noun) the absence of something necessary
accept | except	accept (verb) receive; approve of except (verb) leave out
accurate | precise	In everyday usage, "accurate" and "precise" are considered synonyms. In scientific contexts, however, they are not synonymous. To say that you are less than 10 million years old is accurate (i.e. true) but not precise (i.e. specific). To say that you are 3278 days old would be precise, though not necessarily accurate. If you really are that many days old, then the characterization is both accurate and precise.
ad | add	"Add" is a verb. "Ad" is short for "advertisement."
adapt | adopt	adapt (verb) to make suitable; to become adjusted

	adopt (verb) to assume, take up, or follow
adverse | averse	adverse (adjective) opposing; unfavorable
	averse (adjective) disliking; disinclined
advert | avert	advert (verb) refer
	avert (verb) turn away; prevent
	Example:
	In my speech, I adverted to many famous people.
	I averted my eyes from the bright light.
advice | advise	advice (noun) guidance
	advise (verb) to offer advice
affect | effect	affect (verb) to act on; to have an effect on
	effect (noun) the consequence of a cause; (verb) to cause; to bring about
	Example: I wish to effect several changes that will affect the outcome of our plans.
	The effects of the changes will be beneficial.
affection | affectation	affection (noun) fondness
	affectation (noun) artificial behavior intended to impress others
aggravate | irritate	aggravate (verb) to make worse
	irritate (verb) (1) to annoy or anger (2) to cause inflammation
	"Aggravate" can be used informally to mean "irritate," but we recommend restricting its usage to "worsen," which is its primary meaning.
agree to | agree with	"Agree to" means "consent to."
	"Agree with" means "be consistent with."
	Example:
	I agree to your demands.
	I agree with your opinion.
aid | aide	aid (verb) assist; (noun) assistance
	aide (noun) an assistant
all ready | already	"All ready" conveys the idea of complete readiness.
	already (adverb) previously
	Example:
	We are all ready.
	After I fix this, it will be all ready to go.
	Someone already fixed it.
all right	Always write the expression as two words.
alleged, accused, suspected	These terms, common in news reporting, do little to mitigate the severity of an accusation, and they provide no legal protection for an author. Technically, an accused or suspected murderer is still a murderer — just one that is accused or suspected. Describing someone as "accused of murder" would be more accurate.
	Also, do not speak of the victims of some unidentified criminal as "alleged victims." They are unquestionably victims. The uncertainty lies in the identity of the criminal.
allude | elude	allude (verb) to refer indirectly
	elude (verb) to escape or avoid

	"Allude" and "refer" are not synonymous. To allude is to refer indirectly.
allusion | illusion	allusion (noun) an indirect reference
	illusion (noun) a misleading perception
alternate | alternative	alternate (verb) to occur repeatedly in turn; (noun) a substitute
	alternative (noun) a possibility of several
altogether | all together	"Altogether" means "completely" or "extremely." "All together" means "as one."
alumnus | alumna | alumni | alumnae	"Alumnus" and "alumni" are the singular and plural male forms, respectively. "Alumna" and "alumnae" are the singular and plural female forms, respectively.
ambiguous | ambivalent	ambiguous (adjective) having more than one interpretation
	ambivalent (adjective) simultaneously possessing conflicting opinions
amend | emend	amend (adverb) to make small improvements
	emend (verb) to remove mistakes from a text
amiable | amicable	"Amiable" means "friendly" and describes someone's manner.
	"Amicable" means "peaceful" and usually describes an arrangement or agreement.
among | between	among (preposition) surrounded by or in the midst of; related to some members of a group
	"Between" indicates relationship or combination involving more than one entity.
	Example:
	Search for them among the trees.
	We have plenty of supplies between the five of us.
	Great respect exists between the 10 teammates. (Each person greatly respects every other one.)
	Great respect exists among the 10 teammates. (Some of the teammates show great respect.)
	The cooperation between managers and directors has improved. (The sentence describes a relationship between two groups.)
	The cooperation among managers and directors has improved. (The sentence describes the cooperation within a single group encompassing both managers and directors.)
amoral | immoral	amoral (adjective) lacking moral awareness or concern
	immoral (adjective) evil
amount | number	Use "amount" with something thought of as a whole (e.g. "the amount of information"); use "number" with things considered individually (e.g. "the number of participants").
and/or	This term, meaning "both or exactly one of two," is often used when "or" is sufficient.
anniversary	"Anniversary" refers to the date on which something occurred and is annual by definition. "Five-year anniversary" is redundant (say "fifth anniversary" instead), and "six-month anniversary" makes no sense.
ante- | anti-	"Ante-" means "before."
	"Anti-" means "opposed."
anticipate | expect	anticipate (verb) to prepare for and be aware of
	expect (verb) to regard as likely
anxious | eager	anxious (adjective) nervous or uneasy
	eager (adjective) wanting strongly
appraise | apprise	appraise (verb) to evaluate
	apprise (verb) to inform
apt | likely	"Apt" refers to tendency. "Likely" refers to probability. A person can be apt to do something without being likely to do it.

as far as | as for	"As far as" requires a subject and a verb; "as for" does not. Wrong: As far as the weather, we should be fine. Right: As far as the weather is concerned, we should be fine. Right: As for the weather, we should be fine.
as such	Make sure that "as such" refers to something logical. Right: The waterfall proved to be a large obstacle; as such, it prevented us from going further. ("As such" means "as an obstacle.") Wrong: The waterfall looked dangerous; as such, we didn't go near it. (The waterfall is the only thing "as such" can refer to. The second half of the sentence actually means "we, as the waterfall, didn't go near the waterfall." Replace "as such" with "thus" or "therefore.")
as to	Many find this term pretentious. Use "about" instead. Say "we wondered about their reliability," not "we wondered as to their reliability."
as...as	Wrong: The new model can accelerate more than twice as quickly to 100 miles per hour than the old model. Right: The new model can accelerate more than twice as quickly to 100 miles per hour as the old model. Wrong: People that smoke are more than 10 times as likely to develop lung cancer than people that don't smoke. Right: People that smoke are more than 10 times as likely to develop lung cancer as people that don't smoke.
ascent | assent	ascent (noun) a climb or rise assent (noun) expression of approval or concurrence
assignment | assignation	assignment (noun) (1) the act of allocating or delegating (2) an assigned task or responsibility assignation (noun) a secret plan to meet
assume | presume	assume (verb) to believe without proof presume (verb) take for granted "Presume" connotes arrogance and impertinence. The adjective "presumptuous" means "not recognizing what is permissible or appropriate."
assure | ensure | insure	assure (verb) to inform confidently ensure (verb) to make certain of insure (verb) to protect with insurance
astrology | astronomy	Astrology is a form of fortune telling. Astronomy is a branch of physics.
attorney | lawyer	attorney (noun) a person appointed to act for another in legal or business matters lawyer (noun) a person that practices law An attorney is often (but not necessarily) a lawyer.
bad | badly	"Bad" is an adjective and describes nouns. "Badly" is an adverb and describes verbs or modifiers. Example: I felt bad about what happened. I badly injured my arm.
bare | bear	bare (verb) to expose bear (verb) to support; to bring forth; to put up with

	You can bear a burden, and a tree can bear fruit. A wolf can bare its fangs. "Bear with me" means "put up with me." "Bare with me" means something entirely different.
barter | haggle	barter (verb) to exchange goods or services without involving money
	haggle (verb) to bargain persistently
bated breath	The correct word is "bated" (as in "abated"), not "baited."
bazaar | bizarre	bizarre (adjective) strange
	A bazaar is a kind of shop.
be sure to	"Be sure to practice" means "make sure you practice." "Be sure and practice" means "practice and also be certain."
beg the question	To beg the question is to assume the very point you are trying to prove. For instance, "the universe could not have come from nothing, because only nothing can come from nothing" begs the question. In order to prove that the universe cannot come from nothing, the argument assumes that something cannot come from nothing, which is the point being debated in the first place. "Assuming the conclusion" and "circular reasoning" are much clearer terms for this sort of argumentation. A lot of people will be confused if you call circular reasoning "begging the question." Many use "beg the question" to mean "raise the question." They are better off saying "raise the question" or "lead to the question" instead, both of which are much clearer. Using "beg the question" to mean "raise the question" will offend those that understand it to mean "assume the conclusion" and cause them to brand the user as a careless, ignorant person. In short, "beg the question" is a hopelessly unclear phrase that you should never use. It will confuse or annoy a lot of people, so just say "circular reasoning" or "raise the question," depending on what you mean.
being that, being as	Many find these terms pretentious. Use "because" instead — it's more concise anyway.
belie	belie (verb) fail to give a true notion of
bemuse | amuse	bemuse (verb) to confuse
	amuse (verb) to entertain; to make (a person) laugh
benefactor | beneficiary	A beneficiary receives benefits from a benefactor.
berth	berth (noun) (1) the assigned place of a ship at a dock or wharf (2) a bunk on a train or ship For some strange reason, sports commentators talk about securing "playoff berths" when "playoff spots" would be far clearer (and more sensible).
beside | besides	beside (preposition) next to
	besides (preposition) in addition to; (adverb) additionally Example: Besides, no one besides me is beside you.
bimonthly	You're better off saying "twice a month" or "every two months," depending on what you mean. Using "bimonthly" will end up causing a lot of confusion. Avoid it, along with "biweekly," "biannually," and "biennially."
both	both (modifier, pronoun) one and the other "Both" applies to exactly two what can apply to one. It should be used only with descriptions that could apply to one thing.

Wrong: Both have something in common. (One thing cannot "have something in common." The sentence suggests that each has something in common with a third, unspecified entity.)

Right: They have something in common.

Wrong: Both professors disagree on how to interpret the data. (Apparently, the two professors disagree with someone else, not each other.)

Right: Each professor disagrees with the other.

Right: The two professors disagree with each other.

Wrong: It applies both to children as well as adults.

Right: It applies to children as well as adults.

Right: It applies to both children and adults.

Wrong: It is both efficient, portable, and effective. ("Both" should not be used with more than two.)

Right: It is efficient, portable, and effective.

"Both" can be confusing and is often unnecessary; don't use it if you don't have to. In many situations, "each" is a better choice.

Unclear: We both received $20. (What is the total amount received?)

Clear: We received $20. ($20 total)

Clear: We each received $20. ($40 total)

Awkward: Both paintings are the same.

Better: The paintings are the same.

Awkward: Both praised the other.

Better: Each praised the other.

Better: They praised each other.

Wordy: It applies to both children and adults.

Better: It applies to children and adults.

To indicate possession with the pronoun "both," use the preposition "of."

Wrong: both's belief

Right: the belief of both

brunt	brunt (noun) the main force of something
burglary | robbery	burglary (noun) unlawful entry with the intent to steal
	robbery (noun) the act of taking by force
burst | bust	burst (verb) to explode or break apart
	bust (noun) a sculpture depicting the shoulders, chest, and head of a human
by | bye | buy	"By" is a preposition.
	"Bye" refers to the transfer of a competitor to the next level of a tournament in the absence of an opponent. It is also an abbreviation for "goodbye."
	"Buy" is either a verb or a noun meaning "purchase."
cache | cachet	cache (noun) a hidden store of valuables (pronounced like "cash")
	cachet (noun) prestige; an indication of approval or superiority (pronounced "ca-shay")
callous | callused	callous (adjective) insensitive
	callused (adjective) having hardened skin
Calvary | cavalry	"Calvary" is the name of a hill near Jerusalem.
	cavalry (noun) soldiers that fight on horseback or in armored vehicles

can't help	An action you can't help is one you must carry out. "I can't help wondering" means "I can't resist wondering" or "I am forced to wonder." Don't say "I can't help but wonder," which contains an extra negative word. "But" is at best redundant; at worst, it causes the sentence to express the opposite of what was intended.
can't...too	Sentences such as "you can't sleep too much" are ambiguous. Instead, say "sleeping too much is impossible" or "you shouldn't sleep too much," depending on your intended meaning.
canon | cannon	canon (noun) a general rule or standard cannon (noun) a large gun "Canon" also refers to a kind of music.
canvas | canvass	canvas (noun) a heavy, strong, closely woven fabric canvass (verb) to survey; to determine people's opinions by asking them questions
carat | caret | carrot | karat	carat (noun) (1) a unit of weight for precious stones (2) a measure of the purity of gold caret (noun) a proofreader's mark indicating where something should be inserted A carrot is a vegetable. "Carat" is sometimes spelled "karat."
catholic	If it's capitalized, the word means "of Roman Catholicism." If it's lowercase, the word means "broad" or "wide-ranging."
cement | concrete	Concrete is a combination of cement, sand, gravel, and water. Cement is a gray powder.
censor | censure | sensor | censer	censor (verb) to suppress unacceptable content censure (noun) harsh criticism sensor (noun) a device used for detection censer (noun) a container incense is burned in
censure | criticize	censure (verb) to express disapproval criticize (verb) to indicate faults; to assess
ceremonial | ceremonious	ceremonial (adjective) related to or used for a ceremony ceremonious (adjective) formal
childlike | childish	childlike (adjective) demonstrating or resembling the good qualities of a child, such as ingenuousness childish (adjective) immature
choose | chose	"Chose" is the past form of "choose."
chute | shoot	chute (noun) a sloping channel shoot (verb) to emit suddenly and forcefully; (noun) a branch
cite | site | sight	cite (verb) to reference site (noun) the area something is located on sight (noun) the ability to see; something that can be seen Also, the term is "sightseeing," not "siteseeing."
classic | classical	classic (adjective) (1) of the highest quality (2) typical classical (adjective) related to ancient Greece or ancient Rome
cliché | clichéd	Something containing clichés is clichéd.
climatic | climactic	climatic (adjective) related to prevailing, long-term weather conditions climactic (adjective) forming a climax
coarse | course	coarse (adjective) lacking refinement; rough course (verb) to move along quickly; (noun) a route or direction
collaborate | corroborate	collaborate (verb) to work together

	corroborate (verb) to support, strengthen, or confirm
coma | comma	coma (noun) a prolonged state of deep unconsciousness
	A comma is a punctuation mark.
common | commonplace	common (adjective) occurring often
	commonplace (adjective) ordinary; unoriginal; trite
common | mutual	common (adjective) shared
	mutual (adjective) having the same relationship to each other; reciprocal
	"We have a common dislike" means we dislike the same thing. "We have a mutual dislike" means we dislike each other.
compare to | compare with	Comparing something to something else involves describing similarities. Comparing something with something else involves describing similarities and differences.
	"Compare and contrast with" is redundant. "Compare with" is sufficient.
complement | compliment	complement (noun) an addition, enhancement, or improvement
	compliment (noun) an expression of praise
comprehensible | comprehensive	comprehensible (adjective) able to be understood
	comprehensive (adjective) all-inclusive
comprise | compose	comprise (verb) to consist of
	compose (verb) to constitute
	Wrong: A football team is comprised of football players.
	Right: A football team is composed of football players.
	Right: A football team comprises football players.
	Right: Football players compose a football team.
compulsion | compunction	compulsion (noun) an irresistible urge
	compunction (noun) a feeling of guilt
confidant | confident	confidant (noun) a trusted friend
	confident (adjective) feeling confidence or certainty
congenital | congenial	congenital (adjective) present since birth
	congenial (adjective) pleasingly similar; apt to one's taste
connotation | denotation	A word's denotation is its literal meaning. A word's connotation is its implied meaning.
conscience | conscious | consciousness	conscience (noun) a person's moral sense
	conscious (adjective) having awareness; intentional
	consciousness (noun) a state of awareness
consensus	consensus (noun) general agreement
	This word is not spelled like "census."
	Do not say "general consensus" or "consensus of opinion," both of which are redundant. "Consensus" is sufficient.
consider	When used to mean "believe to be," "consider" should not be followed by "as."

	Wrong: We consider that action as helpful.
	Right: We consider that action helpful.
contemptible | contemptuous	contemptible (adjective) deserving disdain
	contemptuous (adjective) scornful
continual | continuous	continual (adjective) occurring frequently
	continuous (adjective) uninterrupted
converse | inverse	"Converse" involves transposition. The converse of the statement "if A then B" is "if B then A." "I love you" is the converse of "you love me." "Inverse" involves negation. The inverse of addition is subtraction. The inverse of the statement "if A then B" is "if not A then not B." Knowledge and ignorance are inversely related.
core | corps | corpse	core (noun) the central or most significant part
	corps (noun) a group of people
	corpse (noun) a dead body
could not care less	"I could care less" means that I am capable of caring less. Therefore, the sentence implies that I must care to some degree. If I am trying to say that I do not care at all, then I should say "I could not care less."
	Some insist that "I could care less" is justifiable as an ironic statement. Even if they are right, people are better off expressing the irony with more forceful, less convoluted expressions.
councilor | counselor	councilor (noun) a member of a council
	counselor (noun) an advisor
counsel | council | consul | console	counsel (noun) advice
	council (noun) a group of individuals selected to make decisions or discuss matters
	consul (noun) the local representative of a foreign government
	console (noun) a panel of controls
	console (verb) to comfort
credible | credulous | creditable	credible (adjective) believable
	credulous (adjective) too readily willing to believe
	creditable (adjective) worthy of acknowledgment, though not necessarily excellent
crumble | crumple	crumble (verb) to fall apart into small pieces
	crumple (verb) to become or cause to be wrinkled as a result of being crushed
cue | queue	cue (noun) a signal
	queue (noun) a sequence
currant | current	A currant is a fruit.
	current (noun) a flow of electricity, water, or air; (adjective) happening in the present
deadly | deathly	deadly (adjective) lethal
	deathly (adjective) like death
	Poison is deadly. Silence is deathly.
decent | descent | dissent	decent (adjective) appropriate; satisfactory; accepted; respectable
	descent (noun) (1) a downward movement (2) a person's origin
	dissent (noun) disagreement
deduce | deduct	deduce (verb) conclude logically
	deduct (verb) subtract

defuse | diffuse	defuse (verb) to negate the danger of
	diffuse (verb) to disperse over a large area
deprecate | depreciate	deprecate (verb) to express disapproval
	depreciate (verb) to lessen the value of something
desert | dessert	desert (noun) a desolate land; (verb) to abandon
	dessert (noun) the final course of a meal
desirable | desirous	desirable (adjective) worth having or seeking
	desirous (adjective) having desire for something
device | devise	device (noun) an instrument
	devise (verb) to come up with
devote | devout	devote (verb) to set aside or dedicate
	devout (adjective) earnest; devoted
die | dye	die (verb) to stop functioning
	dye (noun) a substance used for coloring
differ from | differ with	To differ from is to be unlike.
	To differ with is to disagree.
different	Instead of saying "I am different than you," say "I am different from you." Using "different" with "than" is likely to draw heavy criticism because "than" is usually not used with non-comparative words (a prominent exception being "other than"). Expressions such as "it is different than that" and "it is superior than that" make about as much sense as "it is old than that."
	"From" cannot be used with elements that do not function as nouns, so saying something like "it works differently than it used to" is acceptable, though you might want to say "it works differently from the way it used to" instead.
	When using "different," be sure not to make an illogical contrast. "We practice differently from them" senselessly contrasts "we practice" and "them." Instead, say "we practice differently from the way they practice" or "how we practice is different from how they practice."
	Wrong: The rules were different than today.
	Right: The rules were different from today's.
differential	"Differential," which can mean "difference," also has several specific technical meanings. When the simpler word "difference" will do, using "differential" is unnecessary as well as pretentious. Don't speak of a "two point differential" in the score or a "five second differential" between the shot clock and the game clock.
dilatory	dilatory (adjective) stalling intentionally; slow
discover | invent	Existing things are discovered. Created things are invented.
	Computers were invented. Electrons were discovered.
discreet | discrete	discreet (adjective) careful
	discrete (adjective) separate
disinterested | uninterested	disinterested (adjective) impartial; unbiased
	uninterested (adjective) not concerned; indifferent
	Many use "disinterested" to mean "uninterested," so you might want to stay away from the two words entirely. Use "impartial" instead of "disinterested," and use "indifferent" instead of "uninterested." Everyone will know what you mean, and no one will argue with you.

dispassionate	dispassionate (adjective) rational
	This word is not synonymous with "passionless."
dispose | dispose of	dispose (verb) to incline toward or arrange
	"Dispose of" means "get rid of."
dissemble | disassemble	dissemble (verb) to disguise one's motives
	disassemble (verb) to take apart
dock | pier | wharf	dock (noun) an enclosed area of water where ships rest
	pier (noun) a structure leading out to sea, usually used for unloading cargo
	A wharf is like a pier but runs along the shore instead of out to sea.
dual | duel	dual (adjective) consisting of two
	duel (noun) a formal contest between two entities
due to | because of	"Due to" is for describing nouns; "because of" is for describing verbs. This distinction seems unnecessary to us, but some people will complain if you mix these expressions up.
	Example:
	Their victory was due to their brilliant strategy. ("Due to their brilliant strategy" modifies the noun "victory.")
	They won because of a brilliant strategy. ("Because of a brilliant strategy" modifies the verb "won.")
e.g. | i.e.	"E.g." introduces an example. "I.e." introduces an elaborative statement.
each other, one another	Don't write "each other" as one word. Avoid using "each other" and "one another" as subjects. The possessive forms are "each other's" and "one another's."
	Example:
	Awkward: You and I think each other is better.
	Better: You and I each think the other is better.
	Better: Each of us thinks the other is better.
earth, moon	When used as names, the words should be capitalized. Otherwise, they should be lowercase. When "earth" is lowercase, it means "soil."
	Example:
	The Earth is the third planet from the sun.
	Will the Moon ever be colonized?
	The Earth is not the only planet that has a moon.
	We must dig up the earth in this area.
economic | economical	economic (adjective) related to economics or the economy
	economical (adjective) using minimal resources
egoist | egotist | narcissist	Egoists believe that self-interest is the foundation of morality.
	Egotists are conceited, self-absorbed people.
	Narcissism is fascination with or admiration of one's own appearance.
either	Don't use "either" to mean "each." Use "each."
	Example:

	Write your name on either side of the paper. (Write your name on exactly one side. Which side is up to you.)
	Write your name on each side of the paper. (Write your name twice.)
elegy | eulogy	elegy (noun) a mournful poem
	eulogy (noun) a work that praises a person
elicit | illicit	elicit (verb) to bring out; evoke
	illicit (adjective) illegal
else	An indefinite pronoun followed by "else" is made possessive by making "else" possessive (e.g. "somebody else's idea").
emigrate | immigrate	emigrate (verb) to leave one's country with the intent of living in another
	immigrate (verb) to settle in a foreign country
eminent | imminent | immanent	eminent (adjective) distinguished
	imminent (adjective) soon to occur
	immanent (adjective) existing within
endemic | epidemic | pandemic	endemic (adjective) regularly found among a population
	epidemic (noun) an abrupt, pervasive occurrence
	pandemic (adjective) regularly found in a large part of the world
enervate | energize	enervate (verb) to deprive of energy
	energize (verb) to give energy to
enormity | enormousness	enormity (noun) (1) a terrible crime or sin (2) hugeness
	enormousness (noun) hugeness
	Remember that "enormity" does not exclusively mean "hugeness." Use "enormousness" rather than "enormity" to express immensity.
envelop | envelope	envelop (verb) to enclose
	envelope (noun) a container used to enclose a letter
epitaph | epithet | epigram | epigraph | epilogue	epitaph (noun) the inscription on a tombstone
	epithet (noun) something that expresses a characteristic attribute
	epigram (noun) a short, witty remark or poem
	epigraph (noun) the inscription on a statue; the quotation at the beginning of a book or chapter, intended to suggest its subject or thesis
	epilogue (noun) something that makes concluding comments at the end of a work
et cetera (etc.)	"Et cetera" is Latin for "and the rest." Don't say "and et cetera," and don't spell the abbreviation "ect." The correct abbreviation consists of the first three letters of the expression. Don't use this expression if you yourself can't think of anything else to add to your list.
	Right: one, two, three, etc.
	Wrong: Everyone will benefit — children, adolescents, adults, etc.
ethereal | ephemeral	ethereal (adjective) insubstantial and delicate; ghostly
	ephemeral (adjective) short-lived
etymology | eschatology | epistemology |	etymology (noun) a description of the history of an expression
	eschatology (noun) the part of theology concerned with death, divine judgment, and the end of the world
	epistemology (noun) the philosophical study of knowledge

etiology | ethology | entomology	etiology (noun) (also spelled "aetiology") the cause of a disease ethology (noun) the science of behavior entomology (noun) the study of insects
evoke | invoke	evoke (verb) to call forth or summon invoke (verb) to resort to, call upon, or appeal to
exalt | exult	exalt (verb) to praise or honor exult (verb) to feel or express happiness
exasperate | exacerbate	exasperate (verb) to irritate exacerbate (verb) to make a bad thing worse
exceptional | exceptionable	exceptional (adjective) unusual in degree exceptionable (adjective) objectionable
exorcise | exercise	exorcise (verb) to drive out or remove exercise (verb) to improve fitness or understanding; to use
fact	Do not call opinions facts, however widely held those opinions may be.
fair | fare	fair (adjective) impartial; legitimate; (noun) a gathering for entertainment, exhibition, or the sale of goods fare (verb) proceed; turn out; (noun) (1) the fee for public transportation (2) typical food and drink
false sense of hope, security, etc.	People that mistakenly feel hopeful experience a "false sense of hope," not "a sense of false hope."
faze | phase	faze (verb) to disturb phase (noun) a distinct state or stage within a process
feckless	feckless (adjective) irresponsible
feint | faint	feint (noun) a deceptive maneuver faint (adjective) lacking clarity, conviction, or strength
felicitous | fortuitous | fortunate	felicitous (adjective) appropriate fortuitous (adjective) occurring by chance; unintentional fortunate (adjective) lucky
first, second, etc.	We recommend the adjectival forms over the adverbial forms (e.g. "firstly," "secondly") when constructing a list.
flare | flair	flare (noun) a burst of light flair (noun) natural talent; elegance
flaunt | flout	flaunt (verb) to display pretentiously or ostentatiously flout (verb) to disregard contemptuously
flotsam | jetsam	flotsam (noun) wreckage found afloat jetsam (noun) things thrown from a ship that have washed ashore
forceful | forcible	forceful (adjective) powerful forcible (adjective) done by force
former | latter	former (adjective) the first mentioned of two latter (adjective) the second mentioned of two If more than two things are involved, use "first" and "last."
forward | foreword	"Forward" is a direction. A foreword is an introduction.
founder | flounder	founder (verb) to sink, fail, or fall flounder (verb) to struggle clumsily

from...to	This construction should define a logical range. For example, "from the Stone Age to the Information Age" defines a range of time, and "from A to R" defines a range of letters. When used properly, the expression will imply examples beyond those listed; for instance, the Bronze Age falls between the Stone Age and the Information Age, and "M" falls between "A" and "R."
	Using "from...to" merely to list specific examples is sloppy and unnecessary. For example, suppose someone says that a book covers "a range of areas, from hurricanes to baseball to the stock market." Can you tell what the book addresses beyond the three topics listed? Probably not, because hurricanes, baseball, and the stock market do not form any sort of sensible range. "Numerous areas, including hurricanes, baseball, and the stock market" is much better.
fulsome	fulsome (adjective) marked by excessive flattery
giant, enormous	Don't fuse "giant" and "enormous," two words that already mean "very large." Both words have plenty of synonyms; there is no need to make one up.
good | well	"Good" is an adjective or a noun; "well" is an adverb. However, "well" can be used as an adjective when describing health.
	Wrong: I slept good.
	Right: I slept well.
	Right: Are they good?
	Right: Are they well? (This is a question about health.)
	Right: They are doing good. ("Good" is a noun that means "that which is right.")
	Right: They are doing well.
got	Don't use "get" or its forms to mean "have." Use "have."
	Example:
	Wordy: I have got to figure this out.
	Better: I have to figure this out.
	Better: I must figure this out.
	Wordy: I have got some spare equipment.
	Better: I have some spare equipment.
	Unnecessary use of "get" is often disguised by a contraction.
	Wrong: I've got some spare equipment.
	The forms of "get" can correctly be used in the sense of "receive," "obtain," "achieve," or "become."
	Example:
	I got a promotion.
	I got to go skydiving.
	I got tired of overworking.
grisly | grizzly	grisly (adjective) causing horror
	A grizzly is a kind of bear.
had ought	"Had" means "must"; "ought" means "should." "Had ought" doesn't mean much of anything.
hang	Use "hanged" as the past and past participle when speaking of capital punishment. Otherwise, use "hung" as the past and past participle.
harebrained	harebrained (adjective) rash; foolish

	The first part of the word is "hare," not "hair."
heal | heel	heal (verb) to make healthy or become healthy
	heel (noun) the back part of a foot or shoe
healthful | healthy	healthful (adjective) giving health
	healthy (adjective) in good health
	A healthful diet leads to a healthy body. A healthful plant will benefit you if you eat it. A healthy plant isn't sick.
hear | here	hear (verb) to perceive sound
	"Here" means "this place" or "in this place."
help the problem	Don't say you want to "help the problem" if you actually want to "help solve the problem." On a related note, "alcoholism support groups" should really be "sobriety support groups."
heroin | heroine	Heroin is a drug.
	heroine (noun) a woman possessing heroic qualities
historic | historical	historic (adjective) important or famous in history
	historical (adjective) having taken place in reality
	Everything that has ever happened is historical. Only a few things are historic.
hoard | horde	hoard (noun) a store of valuables; (verb) to amass valuables
	horde (noun) a large crowd
hole | whole	hole (noun) an opening or depression
	whole (adjective) complete
home | hone	You "home in" on a target, but you hone your skills. To hone is to sharpen.
hopefully, thankfully	"Hopefully" technically means "with hope," but it is widely used to mean "it is hoped." Though common, such usage is sometimes criticized for being nonsensical or vague.
	Example: We will hopefully compete for the championship. (Are we hoping to compete, or will we compete in a hopeful manner?)
	Even if it unambiguously means "it is hoped," "hopefully" still does not specify who is hoping. You can argue that "hopefully" can be used as a sentence modifier, but you're better off finding a clearer, less contentious way of expressing yourself. Instead of "hopefully, I pass my examination," say "I hope I pass my examination" or "let's hope I pass my examination."
	Similarly, "thankfully" is often used illogically, as in "thankfully, the blizzard ended." The blizzard cannot be thankful. "Fortunately, the blizzard ended" makes more sense.
however	To prevent misreading, place a comma after "however" if you use it as a sentence modifier.
hypercritical | hypocritical	Hypercritical people are excessively critical. Hypocritical people pretend to be virtuous.
idea | ideal	idea (noun) a thought
	ideal (adjective) perfect; (noun) a standard or principle
idle | idol	idle (adjective) inactive
	idol (noun) an excessively adored entity
ignorant | stupid	ignorant (adjective) uneducated
	stupid (adjective) lacking intelligence
impeach	impeach (verb) to accuse formally
implicit | explicit	implicit (adjective) implied; indirectly expressed
	explicit (adjective) stated directly and unambiguously

imply | infer	imply (verb) suggest infer (verb) deduce
incidence | incidents | instances	incidence (noun) the degree of occurrence of something "Incidents" is the plural form of "incident," which means "occurrence." Instances are examples.
incredible | incredulous	incredible (adjective) difficult to believe incredulous (adjective) unwilling to believe "Incredible" is often informally used to mean "extremely good."
infamous	infamous (adjective) famous for something bad; notorious
ingenious | ingenuous	ingenious (adjective) clever; creative ingenuous (adjective) innocent; unsuspecting
insidious | invidious	insidious (adjective) operating in a gradual, subtly harmful way invidious (adjective) prejudiced; unfair
insight | incite	insight (noun) clear understanding or perception incite (verb) to provoke or urge
install | instill	install (verb) to place or set up instill (verb) to establish gradually or impart gradually
instances | instants	Instances are examples. Instants are brief moments.
intense | intensive	intense (adjective) of extreme force intensive (adjective) extremely thorough
intermural | intramural | extramural	intermural (adjective) between institutions intramural (adjective) within an institution extramural (adjective) outside the boundaries of an institution
intrigue	intrigue (noun) the scheming of something sinister
invaluable	This term means "extremely valuable," not "worthless."
ironic	Irony involves an incongruity between what is expected and what actually occurs. For example, "Tiny" would be an ironic name for a large animal. "I'm really nervous" would be an ironic statement if I'm actually calm. "Ironic" should not be used merely to mean "odd," "funny," "interesting," or "coincidental."
its | it's	"Its" is a possessive pronoun. "It's" is a contraction standing for "it is."
-ize	Though many useful verbs do end in "-ize" (e.g. "emphasize," "minimize," "organize," "specialize"), many others are better avoided (e.g. "personalize," "incentivize," "finalize"). Don't use this suffix to invent verbs (e.g. "scenarioize"), especially when simpler, better established alternatives exist.
jack | plug	A plug is inserted into a jack or socket.
jealousy | envy	envy (noun) a resentful longing for that belonging to another jealousy (noun) (1) envy (2) fierce protectiveness or vigilance For example, parents are jealous (not envious) of their children's well-being.
just deserts	Deserts are what a person deserves. It's pronounced like "desserts" (the thing you eat) but spelled like "desert" (a desolate land).
kill | murder	kill (verb) to end; to cause death murder (verb) to kill illegally and intentionally

	According to the NIV, ESV, and NASB, the commandment is "you shall not murder," not "you shall not kill."
kind of, sort of	Don't say "kind of a(n)" (e.g. "that kind of an error is common"). In the expression "kind of error," "error" refers to a class rather than an instance, so placing an article in front doesn't make sense. In any case, leaving out the article results in a more concise expression. Using "kind of" or "sort of" to mean "rather" or "to some extent" (e.g. "the speech was kind of long") is considered informal.
knot (unit of measure)	A knot is a unit of speed equivalent to one nautical mile per hour. "Knots per hour" is a unit of acceleration, so do not use it to describe speed.
last | latest	Use "latest" rather than "last" to imply "most recent but not final." "Last" can mean "latest" as well as "final."
leach | leech	leach (verb) to permeate gradually A leech is a parasitic worm (or anyone that acts like one).
lead | led	lead (rhymes with "bed") (noun) a heavy, elemental metal lead (rhymes with "feed") (verb) to draw along; to be in command of; to cause; to begin with; to be in front of "Led" (rhymes with "bed") is the past form and past participle of the verb "lead."
leave	"Leave" doesn't mean the same thing as "let." "Let it be" means "allow it to be" or "don't disturb it" or "leave it alone." "Leave" means to go away or abandon, so "leave it be" makes no sense.
lend | loan	"Lend" is a verb only; "loan" can be a noun or a verb. Some continue to insist that "loan" can't be a verb, but using it as one has been perfectly acceptable for a long time. Observing the restriction on "loan" isn't necessary, but doing so won't hurt.
lessen | lesson	lessen (verb) to decrease lesson (noun) something learned
let alone	When "let alone" connects two examples, the greater one should follow it. The same goes for the expressions "much less" and "never mind." Right: I'm too tired to walk, let alone run. Wrong: I'm too tired to run, let alone walk. Right: I don't know how to start a car, much less build one. Wrong: I don't know how to build a car, much less start one. Right: I can't afford a new car, never mind a new house. Wrong: I can't afford a new house, never mind a new car.
liable | libel	liable (adjective) (1) held legally responsible (2) at risk of something libel (noun) written defamation
libel | slander	libel (noun) written defamation; (verb) to damage someone's reputation with a written statement slander (noun) spoken defamation; (verb) to damage someone's reputation by speaking
lie | lay	"Lie," as a verb meaning "to be in a resting position," is intransitive. "Lay" is a transitive verb meaning "to place." People become confused because "lay" is also the past form of "lie." The past form of "lay" (the transitive verb) is "laid." If you have trouble deciding between "lie" and "lay" in present time, temporarily use "put" or "place" as the verb instead. If your statement makes sense, then "lay" is the correct verb. Otherwise, "lie" is correct. "Lie" can also mean "to intentionally give a false impression." The past form of this verb is "lied."

like | as	As a preposition, "like" means "similar to" or "in the manner of."

Example:

I greatly respect people like them.
I think I would remember something like that.

When giving examples, use "such as" instead of "like."

Example: activities such as skydiving and rafting

"Activities like skydiving and rafting" means "activities similar to skydiving and rafting."

"Like" often appears in speech as filler. Such usage is a strong indication of poor expression.

Wordy: Do you, like, have a lot of work?
Better: Do you have a lot of work?
Better: Are you busy?
Wordy (and immature): And I was totally like "no way!"
Better: I was in disbelief.

Some insist that "like" can't be a conjunction, though most ignore this pointless restriction. Still, if you want to avoid trouble, don't use "like" to introduce clauses; use "as," "as if," or "as though" instead. However, "like" is accepted if the verb of the clause it introduces is omitted.

Keep in mind that "as" can also be a preposition meaning "in the character or role of." "They act as the supervisors" means "they perform a supervisor's duties." "They act like the supervisors" means "their behavior is similar to that of the supervisors."

Finally, ensure that your comparisons are logical.

Wrong: Have you ever seen people strike a tennis ball like them? (The sentence unintentionally makes a comparison between a tennis ball and people.)
Right: Have you ever seen people strike a tennis ball as they do?

literally | figuratively	Don't use "literally" to describe what is figurative. There are plenty of less questionable ways to emphasize an idea.

Wrong: I literally died of embarrassment.
Right: I almost died from the embarrassment.

loath | loathe	loath (adjective) unwilling loathe (verb) to find disgusting or repugnant
lose | loose	"Lose" is the opposite of "win" and "find." "Loose" is the opposite of "tight."
lustful | lusty	lustful (adjective) driven by strong sexual desire lusty (adjective) strong and healthy
luxurious | luxuriant	luxurious (adjective) gratifying to the senses luxuriant (adjective) abundant; complex
marshal | martial | marital | Marshall	marshal (verb) to arrange logically; to rank; to prepare for action

martial (adjective) relating to war (e.g. martial arts, martial law)

marital (adjective) relating to marriage

A marshal is an officer. "Marshall" is a person's name.

mean | median	In statistics, "mean" is another word for "arithmetic average." The mean and median of a data set do not have to be equal. For example, the mean of the numbers in the set {1, 2, 27} is 10, but the median is 2. Contrary to popular belief, almost all the numbers in a set can be below average.
medal | metal | meddle | mettle	A medal is an award. Metal is a substance. meddle (verb) to intrude in the affairs of another mettle (noun) courage; spirit; resilience
memento	The word is not spelled "momento."
method | methodology	method (noun) a way of doing something methodology (noun) a system of methods followed in a particular field
militate | mitigate	militate (verb) to have powerful influence mitigate (verb) to make less severe
miner | minor	miner (noun) one that works in a mine minor (adjective) having little scope or importance; (noun) a person not of legal age
mistake for	"Mistake as" is almost certainly not what you mean.
moral | morale	moral (adjective) related to right and wrong morale (noun) the perception of well-being; spirit
mortify	mortify (verb) (1) to shame (2) to practice self-denial
mysterious | mystic	mysterious (adjective) inexplicable; baffling mystic (adjective) spiritual
nauseated | nauseous	nauseated (adjective) affected by nausea nauseous (adjective) causing nausea
naval | navel	naval (adjective) related to a navy navel (noun) (1) a scar caused by the detachment of the umbilical cord after birth (2) the center of something
nonplussed	nonplus (verb) confuse; bewilder Stay away from "nonplussed," because many people think it means "calm." You are better off using "calm" or "confused" instead.
nor	"Nor" expresses both negativity and connectivity. Be careful not to construct double negatives with it. Wrong: We cannot advance nor retreat. Right: We cannot advance or retreat. Right: We cannot advance, nor can we retreat. Right: We can neither advance nor retreat.
notoriety	notorious (adjective) famous for something bad notoriety (noun) the state of being notorious Notoriety should not be confused with fame, prominence, importance, distinction, or eminence. Criminals can achieve notoriety or be notorious. Praiseworthy people might achieve notice or notability, but they do not achieve notoriety. They are noteworthy or notable, not notorious.

on one hand	Be sure to balance this expression with "on the other hand." Also, the expression makes sense only if you're comparing two things. Awkward: On one hand, the plot was good, but the acting was not. Better: On one hand, the plot was good. On the other hand, the acting was not.
oncology | ontology	oncology (noun) the branch of medicine dealing with tumors; the study of cancer ontology (noun) the philosophy of existence
onetime | one-time	onetime (adjective) former (e.g. "a onetime football coach") one-time (adjective) on one occasion (e.g. "a one-time expense")
open | unlocked	Don't say "leave the door open" if you actually mean "leave the door unlocked." An unlocked door is not necessarily open.
oppress | repress	oppress (verb) to cause to suffer repress (verb) to restrain, inhibit, or subdue; to suppress
-oriented	Avoid using the suffix to make up words. See the comments for "-ize."
pair | pare | pear	pair (noun) a set of two things regarded as a unit; two things of the same kind; (verb) to form or occur in a pair or pairs; to bring two things together pare (verb) to peel; to trim the edges from; to reduce gradually A pear is a fruit.
party	Don't use this as a synonym for "person" unless there's some compelling reason. Unnecessary: They are the parties responsible. Better: They are the people responsible.
passable | passible	passable (adjective) acceptable; free of obstacle passible (adjective) capable of feeling
pathos | bathos	pathos (noun) a quality that induces compassion bathos (noun) the abrupt appearance of the commonplace in otherwise lofty material
peace | piece	You try to achieve "peace of mind," not "piece of mind." However, you can give someone a "piece of your mind" (i.e. rebuke someone).
peak | peek | pique	peak (noun) the highest point; (verb) to reach the highest point peek (noun) a glance; (verb) to look at briefly pique (verb) stimulate
penultimate	"Penultimate" means "second to last" and should not be used to mean "greater than ultimate," which makes no sense anyway. Many say "penultimate" when they actually mean "quintessential." In case you're wondering, "antepenultimate" means "third to last."
per	per (preposition) (1) for each (2) by means of (3) in accordance with; in response to Writing "as per your request" is unnecessary. "Per your request" correctly expresses the intended meaning.
percentage | percent	percent (noun) one part in every hundred percentage (noun) a rate or proportion expressed in terms of each hundred
periodic | periodical	periodic (adjective) regularly occurring periodical (noun) a periodic publication
persecute | prosecute	persecute (verb) to harass persistently prosecute (verb) to carry out legal action against
plain | plane	plain (noun) a large, flat area of land; (adjective) simple or ordinary; clearly revealed plane (noun) (1) a flat surface determined by three points (2) a level (3) an aircraft with fixed wings (4) a tool for smoothing or shaping wood

podium | lectern	A podium is a raised platform that a speaker stands on. A lectern is a slanted stand used to hold a lecturer's materials.
pore over	pore (verb) to be engrossed in the reading of
	To "pore over" means to ponder. You can pour water over something, but you "pore over" a document.
practical | practicable	practical (adjective) useful in non-theoretical situations
	practicable (adjective) feasible
pray | prey	pray (verb) to say a prayer
	prey (verb) to hunt or exploit; (noun) something hunted; a victim
	A praying mantis is an insect that holds its forelegs in a way that suggests prayer.
precede | proceed	precede (verb) to go before in position or time
	proceed (verb) to begin; to go ahead with
preferable to	One option is "preferable to" another. "Preferable than" makes no sense unless you say something like "A is more preferable to B than C is."
premier | premiere	premier (adjective) first in rank, degree, or position; earliest
	premiere (noun) the first public performance of a show
premise | premises	premise (noun) an assumption
	premises (noun) a building and its associated land
prescribe | proscribe	prescribe (verb) authorize the use of
	proscribe (verb) forbid
presently	Avoid using this vague term, which can mean either "soon" or "now."
prestigious	This word rarely serves any purpose. Prestigious things don't need to be called prestigious. People already know that they are. If people don't know that something is prestigious, it probably isn't.
principal | principle	principal (adjective) of greatest importance; (noun) the head of a school; the most important person of a group
	principle (noun) a fundamental rule, belief, or truth
prodigy | progeny	prodigy (noun) an exceptionally talented person
	progeny (noun) offspring
prone | supine	prone (adjective) lying face downward
	supine (adjective) lying face upward
prophecy | prophesy	"Prophecy" (PRAH-fuh-see) is a noun. "Prophesy" (PRAH-fuh-sigh) is a verb.
prosperity | posterity	prosperity (noun) good fortune; success
	posterity (noun) future generations
prostate | prostrate	The prostate is a gland.
	prostrate (adjective) lying face downward
psychology | psychiatry	psychology (noun) the study of the human mind
	psychiatry (noun) the area of medicine concerned with the diagnosis and treatment of mental disorders
raise | rise	raise (verb) to lift or increase
	rise (verb) to go up
	"Raise" is transitive. "Rise" is intransitive.
rare | scarce	rare (adjective) occurring in small quantities and extremely valuable
	scarce (adjective) inadequate relative to the demand; in short supply

rational | rationale | rationalization	rational (adjective) logical
	rationale (noun) a reason
	rationalization (noun) an attempt to justify something
recent | resent	recent (adjective) not long ago
	resent (verb) to feel indignant about
regime | regimen | regiment	regime (noun) a government
	regimen (noun) systematic therapeutic treatment
	regiment (noun) a military unit
regretful | regrettable	regretful (adjective) feeling regret
	regrettable (adjective) causing regret
remote, close	"Remote" means "distant," so the phrase "not even remotely close" makes no sense (though something can be "not even remotely correct").
respectable | respectful	respectable (adjective) deserving respect
	respectful (adjective) feeling respect
respectfully | respectively	respectfully (adverb) demonstrating respect
	respectively (adjective) separately in the given order
	Example: My cousin and I are an astronaut and a professor, respectively. (My cousin is an astronaut; I'm a professor.)
retch | wretch	retch (verb) to vomit
	wretch (noun) a pitied or despicable person
rhetorical question	A rhetorical question suggests its own answer. It is used to make a point rather than obtain information. Think of a rhetorical question as a declaration constructed as a question.
	Example:
	What could be simpler?
	Are you going to stand there and do nothing?
riffle | rifle	riffle (verb) to shuffle or stir up; to look through written materials
	rifle (verb) to search through without authorization; to loot
	A rifle is also a kind of firearm.
right | rite | write | wright	right (adjective) correct; morally justified; (noun) a legal entitlement
	rite (noun) a ceremony
	write (verb) to compose
	"Right" is also a direction. "Wright" is (1) a surname or (2) an archaic word for "builder."
rightful | right	rightful (adjective) just or legally established
	right (adjective) correct, acceptable, satisfactory, or proper
rouge | rogue	Rouge is a red powder used to color the cheeks.
	rogue (noun) a scoundrel; a mischievous person
select | selected	select (adjective) special; outstanding; chosen as being the best
	"Selected" is the past form of the verb "select," which means "to make a choice."
sensory | sensuous | sensual	sensory (adjective) relating to perception

	sensuous (adjective) affecting the senses, not the intellect
	sensual (adjective) physically gratifying (especially in a sexual sense)
serve | service	serve (verb) to attend to; to perform services for
	service (noun) an act of assistance; the action of serving; (verb) (1) perform maintenance on (2) pay interest on (3) mate with
set | sit	"Set" means "to put or to place something somewhere" or "to put in motion." It is always transitive. "Sit" means "to be in a seated position" or "to be at rest." It is virtually always intransitive. It is transitive if used to mean "have someone sit" (e.g. "we sat them down for a talk").
simple | simplistic	simple (adjective) easily done; uncomplicated
	simplistic (adjective) inappropriately simplified; ignoring complexity
something | somewhat	something (noun) a thing of some kind
	somewhat (adjective) to a moderate degree
stationary | stationery	stationary (adjective) fixed; unmoving
	stationery (noun) writing materials
stood | stayed	"Stood" is the past form of "stand."
	"Stayed" is the past form of "stay."
superior to	"Superior than" makes no sense. One thing is "superior to" another.
supposedly | supposably	supposedly (adverb) reputedly; purportedly; allegedly
	supposably (adverb) capable of being supposed
	You will almost never need to use "supposably."
suspect | suspicious	suspect (noun) someone suspected of a crime; (adjective) possibly dangerous or untrue; (verb) (1) to believe to be probable (2) to believe to be guilty; to regard with suspicion
	suspicious (adjective) (1) distrustful (2) causing suspicion
sympathy | empathy	sympathy (noun) feelings of sorrow for someone else; compassion
	empathy (noun) the understanding and sharing of another's feelings
table	To some, "table" means "bring up for discussion," and to others, it means "postpone discussion of." Many people aren't even aware that "table" can be a verb, so you might want to avoid this usage altogether. Just say "brought up" or "postponed," depending on what you mean.
tack | tact	tack (noun) (1) a small nail with a large head (2) a course of action (3) the direction of a boat relative to the direction of the wind
	tact (noun) skill in dealing with people
than | then | that	"Than" is used in comparison (e.g. "one is taller than the other").
	"Then" expresses time relationships (e.g. "write down and then organize the information").
	"That" is a pronoun, modifier, or conjunction.
theory	Informally, "theory" often refers to speculation. In science, however, a theory is a well-substantiated explanation (e.g. atomic theory, the theory of relativity).
there | their | they're	there (adverb) in that place
	"Their" is a possessive pronoun.
	"They're" is a contraction standing for "they are."
	Wrong: The supplies are in they're. (Expanding the contraction results in "the supplies are in they are," which makes no sense.)
	Right: The supplies are in there.
threw | through	"Threw" is the past form of "throw."

	"Through" is a preposition or an adverb (e.g. "through a tunnel," "through a city").
times smaller, slower, etc.	Phrases such as "2.5 times smaller" and "3 times slower" don't actually make sense. Say "40% as large" and "one third as fast" instead.
tortuous | torturous	tortuous (adjective) twisting; complex torturous (adjective) marked by extreme pain and suffering
try	"Try" takes an infinitive. Don't say "try and" unless you really mean it. "Try to evaluate the new product" and "try and evaluate the new product" have different meanings.
two | to | too	"Two" is the integer greater than one and less than three. "To" is a preposition. "Too" means "also" or "to an undesirable degree."
type	Don't use "type" to mean "kind of." Wrong: That type hat is common. Right: That kind of hat is common.
unique	"Unique" is an absolute adjective — it has no comparative or superlative forms. Something can't be "more unique" or "the most unique."
utilize	"Utilize" means "to make effective use of." "We used all the fuel" could mean that we wasted it. "We utilized all the fuel" means we did something beneficial with it. "Utilize" should not be used as a synonym for "use." Don't say "we utilized a computer to perform the calculations." Instead, say "we used a computer to perform the calculations."
vain | vane | vein	vain (adjective) (1) conceited (2) useless vane (noun) a broad blade that moves or is moved by a fluid or gas "Vein" refers to a strand or layer of something. A vein is also a kind of blood vessel.
venal | venial	venal (adjective) susceptible to bribery venial (adjective) pardonable
verbal | oral	oral (adjective) spoken instead of written; related to the mouth "Verbal" can be a synonym for "oral," but its primary definition is "related to words." Written words are verbal, though they are not oral. Spoken words are both oral and verbal. If your intended meaning is "spoken," then use "oral" rather than "verbal."
verses | versus	"Verses" is the plural form of verse. versus (preposition) against; in contrast to
vest | invest	vest (verb) endow; bestow invest (verb) put money into You pronounce someone husband and wife by the power vested in you, not by the power invested in you.
vice | vise	vice (noun) immoral behavior A vise is a holding device.
vintage | vantage	vintage (noun) the year in which wine was produced vantage (noun) an advantageous location or circumstance
virtually	virtually (adverb) nearly; almost entirely "Virtually" does not mean "genuinely" or "actually." Something "virtually perfect" may still have flaws.
wangle | wrangle	wangle (verb) obtain through manipulation wrangle (verb) to dispute at length
wary | weary	wary (adjective) cautious; watchful weary (adjective) tired; fatigued
weak | week	weak (adjective) lacking strength

	week (noun) a period of seven consecutive days
weather | wether | whether	weather (noun) meteorological conditions wether (noun) a castrated ram "Whether" is a conjunction.
when, where	Do not use "when" in definitions that do not actually involve time, and do not use "where" in definitions that do not actually involve place. Right: China is where fireworks were invented. Wrong: It was the kind of injury where you have to rest for several weeks. Right: It was the kind of injury that forces you to rest for several weeks. Wrong: A spoonerism is where you transpose the beginning sounds of two words. Wrong: When you transpose the beginning sounds of two words, it's called a spoonerism. A spoonerism is not a location, so calling it a "where" makes no sense. And when you transpose the beginning sounds of two words, we doubt anyone actually calls it anything. A spoonerism is a thing, so you could say "a spoonerism is what happens when you transpose the beginning sounds of two words." However, this sentence is still too wordy. Simply say "a spoonerism is the transposition of the beginning sounds of two words." "Where" is often used in situations in which "which" is more appropriate. Wrong: It was a game where nothing interesting happened. Right: It was a game in which nothing interesting happened. Wrong: It is a problem where no solution exists. Right: It is a problem to which no solution exists.
whether | if	Use "if" to introduce conditions, and use "whether" to introduce alternatives. Wrong: We wonder if anything will change. (People do not wonder conditions. They wonder about alternatives.) Right: We wonder whether anything will change.

A.4   Selected vocabulary

abridge (verb) shorten

accomplish (verb) achieve; bring about

acronym (noun) a word formed from the first letters of other words

ambiguous (adjective) open to more than one interpretation; having several meanings

annotation (noun) an explanatory comment added to a text

anxiety (noun) worry; unease

appendix (noun) a collection of supplementary materials found at the end of a book

association (noun) a conceptual relationship or connection

attribution (noun) assigning to a source

awkward (adjective) difficult to deal with or handle; lacking elegance

category (noun) a set of things that share some characteristic

concise (adjective) expressing a lot in few words

considerably (adverb) to a large degree

contrary (adjective) opposed

decipher (verb) to interpret successfully

delimiter (noun) something that determines a boundary

diligence (noun) careful, deliberate effort

disruptive (adjective) causing disturbance or interruption

distinguish (verb) to perceive the differences between

diverse (adjective) incorporating a wide range of types

drought (noun) a shortage of water caused by a lack of rainfall

efficient (adjective) functioning with minimal waste or expense

elaborate (verb) to add details to or explain the meaning of

elliptical (adjective) involving omission of words

emphasize (verb) to stress or give importance to

expression (noun) a word or group of words functioning as a unit

extremely (adverb) to a great degree or extent

fragment (noun) an incomplete piece, usually broken off from something else

humiliate (verb) to damage the dignity or pride of

hypothetical (adjective) based on assumption or thought rather than on fact

immediately (adverb) without delay

impolite (adjective) not demonstrating good manners

incinerate (verb) to burn to ashes

indicative (adjective) pointing out or showing; strongly implying

inflict (verb) to cause or impose something unpleasant

justify (verb) to prove to be right or reasonable

laureate (noun) someone honored for outstanding achievement

monosyllabic (adjective) consisting of one syllable

negation (noun) the act of making something negative; an expression of denial

parenthesis (noun) a qualifying, elaborative, explanatory, or appositional interruption; the symbol *)* or *(,* used to enclose such an interruption

phrase (noun) one or more words functioning as a whole

redundant (adjective) able to be omitted without loss of meaning; superfluous

respectively (adverb) separately and in the order mentioned

rhetorical (adjective) concerned with the effect or appearance of writing or speaking

salutation (noun) a greeting

sequence (verb) to put in a particular order; (noun) an arrangement or order

stammer (verb) to speak with quick, unexpected pauses and repetitions

statement (noun) something set forth, declared, or asserted

suggestion (noun) an idea offered for consideration

superfluous (adjective) unnecessary from being more than required

temporal (adjective) of or related to time

term (noun) a word or group of words used to identify something

tremble (verb) to shake as a result of fear or excitement

villain (noun) an evil person

volition (noun) the act of choosing; a decision made by the will; the power of using one's will

wordy (adjective) expressed in too many words

A.5   Contact information

master.english@gmx.com

http://mjprinceton.wordpress.com

Index

www.ingramcontent.com/pod-product-compliance
Lightning Source LLC
Chambersburg PA
CBHW082134290526
45794CB00008B/3031